YOUNG WRITERS

Spellbound

NORTHAMPTONSHIRE

Poetry Now

YOUNG WRITERS

Edited by Simon Harwin

First published in Great Britain in 1998 by
POETRY NOW YOUNG WRITERS
1-2 Wainman Road, Woodston,
Peterborough, PE2 7BU
Telephone (01733) 230748

HB ISBN 1 86188 824 4
SB ISBN 1 86188 829 5

FOREWORD

In this, our 5th competition year, we are proud to present *Spellbound Northamptonshire*. This anthology represents the very best endeavours of the children from this region.

The standard of entries was high, which made the task of editing a difficult one, but nonetheless enjoyable. The variety of subject matter, creativity and imagination never ceases to amaze and is indeed an inspiration to us all.

This year's competition attracted the highest entry ever - over 46,000 from all over the UK, and for the first time included entries from English speaking children living abroad.

Congratulations to all the writers published in *Spellbound Northamptonshire*. We hope you enjoy reading the poems and that your success will inspire you to continue writing in the future.

CONTENTS

Adele Haddon	20
Matthew Wurr	20
Sandy Barton	21
Kelly Taylor	21
Darren Mills	22
Leanne McCormick	22
Rachel Wilson	23
Andrew Sarjant	24
Katie Powell	24
Maike Hallenga	25
James Murray	25
Kerrie Dunkley	26
Louise Hunter	26
Georgia Berry	27
Leanne Melhuish	27
Lindsay Bradley	28
Simone Joyce	28
Laura Sanders	29
Laurie Shepherd	29
Calvin Jones	30
Kelly Muckelberg	30
Stacey Pfadenhauer	31
Steven Payne	32
Natalie Briggs	32
Anna Hickman	33
Vikki Macefield	33
Carmel Street	34
Steven Higgins	34
Neil Johnson	35
Sian Hardie	36
Samantha Barnes	36
Elliott Prince	37
Chris Osborne	37
Andrew Payne	38
Katie Megan Sales	38
Karen Baguley	39
Daniel Lee	39
Samantha Beames	40

Debbie Asplin	64
Sarah Griffey	64
Amanda Hampson	65
Rachael Clarkson	66
Andrea Byrne	67
Oliver Newton	68

Newton Road Junior School

Laura Brown	69

Northampton High School

Angela Yussuff	69
Katy Blane	70
Kate Greenhalgh	70
Rebecca Ribbans	71
Antonia Stewart	72
Joanne Ayris	73
Gemma Pirnie	74
Katharine Clark	74
Zoe Corbishley	75
Sarah Jennings	76
Charlotte Crosby	76
Victoria Morris	77
Becky Doyle	77
Robyn Notley	78
Katie Allen	79
Alice Moody	80
Jean Mallock	81
Lucy Byrne	82
Emma Panebianco	83
Sarah Rogers	84
Julie Yau	85
Helen Legg	86
Lydia Bartram	86
Chloe Evans	87
Catherine Guillaume	88

Oundle and Laxton Schools

Mike Ridley	88
Roland Burton	89
N Criado-Perez	89
Charles Parker	90
Felix Barnes	91
Chris Parsons	92
Catherine Cross	92
Olly Cooper	93
Gemma Woodrow	94
Siân Gibson	94
Simon Rowley	95
William Sankey	95
Jonathan Thakkar	96
Andrew King	96
Annabel Lewis	97
Rachel Tracy	97
Jacqueline Hill	98
Anna Wheeler	98
Natalie Allan	99
Pippa Stevenson	100
Alaric Shorter	100
Francesca Dickinson	101
John Hart	102
Sonia Sangha	102
Tom Rogerson	103
Rebecca Hill	104
Lucinda Leonard	105
Nicholas Proffitt	106
James Ducker	106
Ben Brown	107
John Saunders	108
Hannah Burch	108
Anna Dawson	109
Joanna Murray	110
Kate Anderson	110
Lya Pfaffli	111
Jane Charlton	112

THE POEMS

They have all been replaced,
By offices and shops,
Once beautiful countryside,
Swarming with cops.

Cars, buses, taxis and bikes,
Have taken the unfortunate place
Of those memorable Sunday family hikes,
Yet still no shame on the councillor's face.

Thomas Paybody (12)
Bishop Stopford School

THE RACE

The adrenalin pumps,
The tension mounts,
The gun fires and for a second everyone
is frozen,
Then we're off.

With only the finish on our minds
we compete for the positions,
Weaving our way between the
competitors,
Pounding the ground,
Splashing through mud,
It all adds to the thrill!

As we come round the last corner the
finish is in sight.
Must keep up the pace . . .

. . . The pace
        The pace
                The pace!

Kathryn Arnold (12)
Daventry William Parker School

GHOSTS AND GHOULS

They're scary at night
But not in the day
Can't see them in the light
It's their own special way!

Some have no heads
Some have no legs
Some scare you in bed
Some look like pegs!

Check in the cupboard,
Check in the drawer,
Check on the ceiling,
Check on the floor.

My life is ending
What do I do?
The ghost is coming
For me and for you.

Some are white
Some are grey
Some are transparent
At night and at day.

Some are nice
Some are kind
Some sing happily
Always in rhyme.

They're scary at night
But not in the day
Can't see them in the light
It's their own special way!

Leanne Walton (13)
Daventry William Parker School

BILLY BOB JOE

Everyone knows Billy Bob Joe,
'Cause he ate ten pies,
In one whole go.

His face is bloated,
His face will pop,
He'll even eat a corner shop.

Everyone knows Billy Bob Joe,
'Cause he ate ten pies,
In one whole go.

His mum and dad are exactly the same,
I'm not surprised they use a crane.

Everyone knows Billy Bob Joe,
'Cause he ate ten pies,
In one whole go.

He frightens the teachers,
He frightens the kids,
His brother asked 'Where's the fridge?'

Everyone knows Billy Bob Joe,
'Cause he ate ten pies,
In one whole go.

In a race he's the best,
He'll run a metre and
            bounce the rest!

Everyone knows Billy Bob Joe,
'Cause he ate ten pies,
In one whole go.

Tony Dip (12)
Daventry William Parker School

THOUGHTS IN MY HEAD

As I look out of the window,
I see the world go rushing by.
Why do they rush so?
I wonder why?

As I peer round the door,
They're moving so slow.
Where are they going?
Oh, where do they go?

As I stare at the wall,
Everything seems dead.
Everything except . . .
    for the thoughts in my head.

Bethany Clabburn (12)
Daventry William Parker School

THE HACK

To fly with the wind,
to gallop with speed,
to sit up high in the cold
winter's breeze.

You have to be brave
you have to be bold,
and jump quite high in
the sharp winter's cold.

I think you may find when
you've finished your hack,
A hot mug of soup when
        you hang up your mac!

Rebecca Turner (12)
Daventry William Parker School

THE TWO COLD SEASONS

While animals hibernate from the cold windy
weather,
The leaves change to red, orange and brown,
While shiny conkers come out of their green
spiky coats,
Children crush on the leaves fallen down.

While trees crispen up from the icy weather,
The icicles glisten as they hang from the roof,
While birds leave to find somewhere warmer,
Children skate on the frozen-over pond.

Emily Allinson (12)
Daventry William Parker School

SOCCER

The twelve o'clock bell rang for tucker.
Me and the lads went out to play soccer.
We'll thrash 'em and bash 'em and throw them around.
We'll stamp and we'll clap and put them to the ground.
There is a boy called Lee Tate he's good at soccer, I mean 'great'.
The girls are always running for the ball even though they
can't kick it at all.
Running round and doing warm-up bits, hot faces and
sweaty armpits.
We're going to beat the others with no fuss,
the score will be 2/1 to *us!*

Beth Raynham (11)
Daventry William Parker School

A Walk In The Night

Darkness and gloom is all around,
I hear nothing, no, not a sound,
Everywhere is clear,
No one is here,
The moon's gazing down,
Its face like a clown,
The night air is fresh and cool,
I wish to dance round like a mad fool,
Everything's so free,
Alone out here with me,
The sky's becoming light,
And the air's warm and bright.

Davina McMahon (13)
Daventry William Parker School

Hot Chocolate

Sitting in my hands,
My personal central heating,
Lifting me to my cocoa cloud,
The smell clouding my senses.

I look down, a swirling mass of bliss.
As I bring the cup to my lips,
A river of chocolate slides down my throat,
Blocking the cold from the world outside.

The last drop is finished, and I return to my senses,
And I am once again back on earth.
But the smell still lingers under my nose,
And I am soon back in my chocolate world.

Sinéad Bevan (12)
Daventry William Parker School

EVACUEE BOY

The little boy stood cold and lonely,
His legs were weak,
He had no idea where he'd be sent to,
The thought of it brought a
tear down his dirty face,
His name tag itched his little neck,
The gas mask got heavier as he waited,
Questions flashed through his mind,
His mum hugged him and pushed him
onto the train,
The last image of his mum upset him,
Her tear-stained face got smaller as
          the train pulled away from the station.

Sarah Ludford (12)
Daventry William Parker School

RYAN

He used to hop around the garden,
Jump over the little wall,
Then onto the plant pot,
There he would sit,
And chew the flowers,
He could run as fast as Linford Christie,
And he always loved a cuddle,
I loved Ryan and he loved me,
My lovely cuddly rabbit,
Has now gone from my life forever.

Leanne Osborne (12)
Daventry William Parker School

A Winter Day

As I step outside I am hit with a hostile
                    barrier of freezing air.
The snow lays there crisp and pure until my single
                    footprint pollutes such an innocent scene.
A flurry of bitter air hits the side of my face
and abruptly brings me back to an icy, frozen world.

The frost on the ground sparkles and glistens as a
single ray of sunlight illuminates the ground.
An icicle hangs from the rooftop, it points like an
accusing finger pointing down, down to the ground.
As I walk around, everywhere I turn it is desolate and
                    there is a strange dead silence!

Jenna Darler (12)
Daventry William Parker School

Alice's Dilemma

She feels alone inside,
does she run?
Or does she hide?
Withdrawn and left out,
Too scared to even walk about.
Should she tell a teacher or two
Or continue to hide in the girls' loo?
They all used to care,
Now all they do is stop and stare.
She feels alone inside,
Does she run?
Or does she hide?

Helen Clucas (12)
Daventry William Parker School

I wish I was a boat,
So I could swim out at sea
I wish I was a kettle
So I could drink lots of tea.

I wish I was something different
But I can't be
So I will have to make do
With me!

Aishling Larkin (12)
Daventry William Parker School

LOVE

Part 1

From the first time I saw you
I knew I adored you.
I tried to let you go but something
didn't want me to.
I would hold you tight all night
and never let you go.
You make me very happy and my
heart is sure to grow.

Part 2

I met you last night and was holding
you tight scared somebody would
whisk you off your feet.
I was scared and unprepared, it was
almost like a nightmare apart from
the fact there was no one there.

Jodi Hart (13)
Daventry William Parker School

FUNFAIR

As I stepped through into the funfair I had a
shiver down my spine.
As I walked alone I saw all of the cobwebs
on the stalls.

I saw people not so happy and they were
staring at me.
I saw people going the other way and I
was on my own.

When I saw nobody I heard the doors
close, I was alone.
Not a sound I heard until a big bang
and I could hear it wherever I went.

I looked around and it was getting cold.
I looked around to see another exit but
I was trapped.

Kerry Lovejoy (12)
Daventry William Parker School

SHARK ATTACK!

Lying in the ocean the sea is calm
All I can see is the sky above me
And all I can hear is the gentle lapping of waves
But then from the terrible deep
Came the animal who haunts our sleep
It came up through the gentle waves
There used to be blue sea now red it stains
And when it finishes what it came to do
It goes back to the deep
And is now looking for *you!*

Philip Curtis (13)
Daventry William Parker School

THESE TIMES

Repeated lies,
How we realise.

All we know is true,
We are here, but we are who?

Can we ever be sure
Of money, personality, who is really poor?

In these times when nothing is tolerated,
The problems we have are simply overrated.

A solution is what we are looking for
            to solve the problems all around.
We hope and pray for this solution but we know
                    it will never be found.

James Watts (12)
Daventry William Parker School

AUSTRALIA

Red sands, blue seas, a typical surfer's paradise,
Parrots squawking, cicadas clicking, dingoes barking
25 degrees and that's just at night!
Bronze bodies, in the scorching sun,
Surfboards ready,
Dry, yellow grass all around,
Up in the trees, the koalas chew the Eucalyptus,
Kanaroos skip and hop, emus stride by,
Snakes slithering, spiders scurrying,
People stare and wonder at the beauty that is *Australia!*

Philip Spry (12)
Daventry William Parker School

OUT AT SCHOOL

As the wind and rain lashes,
Out over the dark cold sea,
The waves as high as can be,
A boat sways from side to side,
And in the morning it may come
in with the tide.

As the waves crash up against the boat,
The crew are on deck in their raincoats,
Steering the boat in the right direction,
Keeping its course to perfection.

The water seeps in through the cracks in the boat,
'Cause of the waves that crashed against it
whilst it was afloat.
The crew are scared and start to yelp,
But no one's around to come and help.

The boat comes in with the tide,
Upon the water each bit rides,
But where is the crew that were out boating?
Are they dead or are they still floating?

The legend is told on November the 4th,
You can see the boat in the north,
The mystery still lies 'Where is the crew?'
But nobody knows . . . *do you?*

Emma Goosey (12)
Daventry William Parker School

MCDONALD'S

Closing time: The clock strikes eight.
I lock the door and bolt the gate,
The workers say 'Cheerio!'
Home they trot, away they go.

At McDonald's no one's there,
(Well no one that we think)
The lights come on, the party starts,
'Everyone have a drink!'

Here they come, the usual pals,
Spooky, death and grim.
All they do is eat my food,
They're neither fat or thin.

Then the clock strikes 5.00 am
The owner then comes in again.
All the ghosts run and hide,
Another usual day.

I think it's a usual day, you see.
It's the money that I gain.
8 o'clock, the restaurant shuts
And the party starts again.

Aaron Williams (12)
Daventry William Parker School

THE SPIDER POEM

Spider, spider on the wall,
What will you eat today?
Where will you cast your springy net?
Around some fat fly, I bet!

Kate Rutt (11)
Daventry William Parker School

THE INVITATION

You are invited to a night of sheer terror,
At a witches' gathering near 'Lake Forever'
All black cats are invited to come,
Please bring with you:

A newt's toe and thumb
A l s o .
A red beetle's stomach,
A hundred dragon scales
P l u s
Twenty-four red devils' tails.

Please attend at the next full moon,
Fly out at midnight on your witch's broom.
We hope to see you arrive
unharmed,

Yours Horribly,

Witch of Macabre!

Lizzie Stewart (13)
Daventry William Parker School

THE BULLY

Nobody likes me,
I'm sitting alone,
You jested and joked me,
I want to go home.

You've pinched and punched me,
Watched me falling,
Nobody cares,
That it's me you're bullying.

I don't care anymore,
They have to know,
Someday soon,
The bruises will show.

You're waiting outside,
For me to come,
But it soon will be over,
I'm telling my mum!

Samantha John (13)
Daventry William Parker School

THE HAUNTED CHIPPY

The chippy is shut on Sunday,
No one's there, unlike on Monday.
The chilling wind whistles through the shop,
The fryer comes on and it's a shock.
The door opens but nobody's there,
From the shadows come the ghosts.
They come to buy their ghostly chips.
The shop is alive with noise,
Packets of chips floating in the air,
The call of 'Three bags of chips,'
Echoes through the shop.
As the clock ticks through the night,
The customers start to leave,
The shop starts to slow down,
As the last ghosts walk out the door.
The door suddenly slams shut,
All the noise stops,
As no one is in the scariest shop!

Shane Radford (12)
Daventry William Parker School

THE SHOP

The shop was still and unfriendly,
There was no noise; it was silent,
They prefer it that way.

I could not see them but I could sense them.
I heard them think, I heard myself think.

They watched me, watched my every move.
I wanted to run away but I was paralysed,
My legs frozen to the ground.

It was them, they had power over my mind,
They wouldn't let go.
Somewhere in the distance a bell tolled twelve times,
I was myself again, I was free.

Adele Haddon (12)
Daventry William Parker School

UNITED

M an United are the greatest.
A ndy Cole.
N icky Butt.
C up or League they'll always win.
H appy this makes me.
E very week I pray they'll win.
S olskjaer, Scholes, or Sheringham.
T hree or four goals a game.
E uropean glory too.
R yan Giggs, the Welsh winger.

U nited are the greatest team.

Matthew Wurr (13)
Daventry William Parker School

UNCLE JIM

I remember all the happy moments of my great Uncle Jim.
Joking around, sitting on his knee and having a laugh.
He passed away sadly on bank holiday in May.
The family were so unhappy.
When my mum found out,
She was sad and tried not to cry.
But you could see the tears fill up in her eyes,
She wouldn't let it out.
The funeral came.
Wonderful Tonight was playing on the bagpipes,
It was his favourite song.
My nan and grandad were crying,
As the coffin lowered down into the mouth of heaven.
I knew I would never see him again,
But the happy moments remain inside me.

Sandy Barton (13)
Daventry William Parker School

LOVE

As deep as the ocean as wide as the sea.
When love collides and then dies it makes me
very unhappy.
When love climbs the highest mountain and
falls into my heart,
I know that love will always be there but it
may break somebody's heart.
I know when love divides then my heart will
break in two.
At night I always think of you and
my dreams will soon come true.

Kelly Taylor (14)
Daventry William Parker School

SPEEDWAY

Fast at the start,
To get to the first long left-hander.
Skidding, sliding, pushing and shoving,
To get into the lead.

The site is jam-packed,
With lots of tents
And caravans round the outsides.

I don't think too much of the smell,
But everybody thinks smoke smell is
very good.

The sounds of the motorbikes
Are like a stampede coming.
The roar of the crowds
As the last
Person comes
Over the line is
Great!

Darren Mills (12)
Daventry William Parker School

THE TEENAGE LOOK

We're proud and selfish,
We're spiteful and stubborn,
We smoke and drink,
Our morals are wrong.
You were never like us!

We're crazy animals,
You're sensible and boring.
We use slang,
'Neva' talk proper English.
We have fun!

We are good and clever,
If you would just take the time.
We are polite and enthusiastic,
Give us a chance.
I bet you were like us!

Leanne McCormick (13)
Daventry William Parker School

THOUGHTS!

What to write?
Confusing words swirling round in my head.
What next?
Words fly across my eyes.
Adrenaline rises higher and higher.
My brain's going to burst with words.
What shall I write?
My fingers tap on the table.
Thinking . . .
The sound of pens, pencils. Tap. Tap.
A silent humming of brains.
My knees jig up and down.
Two minutes is nearly up.
Eyes rolling round and round.
Stop to think.
The words speeding round and round like on a motorway.
Stop! A loud but excited voice came from Mrs Gadsen.
'No writing now. Who wants to read them?'
A swarm of hands shot up.
Pairs of feet sound like a stampede of buffaloes.
Class quietens to listen to 'Thoughts' the poem.

Rachel Wilson (11)
Daventry William Parker School

CHRISTMAS EVE

I sit in bed thinking of
what I might get.
I run to my door.
I put up my stocking.
I jump up and down. Excited.
It's Christmas tomorrow!
I see the glittering lights
Beaming on the window.
I see the snowflakes falling.
Thinking of a white Christmas.
I hear singing coming from the door.
I see my brother rattling the
presents, maybe thinking of what
it might be.
I go to bed early hoping the morning will come.
You see!
This is what Christmas means to *me*.

Andrew Sarjant (11)
Daventry William Parker School

AUTUMN

Autumn has come the nights are drawing in.
The weather is getting colder and the leaves
are changing colour.
I like to kick the leaves as I walk,
Some people do not like autumn but I do.
All the colours are beautiful, all those
reds, browns and caramels.
I hate when it is over and the
                    snowy weather comes

Katie Powell (13)
Daventry William Parker School

TEENAGERS

Some are good,
Some are bad,
Some drive their poor parents mad.

They think they are so cool,
By not going to school.

Some can be really shy,
Some make little children cry.

They always want to
Spend and spend, but,
Have to pay back in the end.

Helpful sometimes, they can be,
By making gran a cup of tea.

They do their homework nice and neat,
To keep their dotty teachers sweet.

Maike Hallenga (13)
Daventry William Parker School

THE GUNNERS

A rsenal the crowd all cheer.
R ay Parlour races through the mid-field,
S eaman makes another great save,
E ncouragement from the manager is
      shouted to the players.
N early another goal from Dutch ace
      Dennis Bergkamp.
A nelka comes on as a sub,
L ast minute of the game and the
                  Gunners are cruising.

James Murray (13)
Daventry William Parker School

STOP BULLYING ME

Why are they so mean to me?
I wish they'd all just let me be.
They beat me up as I got off the bus,
And then they left me in a rush.
A teacher came and pulled me up,
Asking me what it's all about?
I told him what had happened and then,
He said it wouldn't happen again.
But the very next day,
They shoved me in a pile of hay.
They said don't tell of us again,
Or you'll be in a great deal of pain.
When I got home my mother said,
'I'd better have a word with the head.'
The bullies got suspended for 10 days,
And told they must end their ways.
But I know that'll do no good,
I'll still end up in a pool of blood.

Kerrie Dunkley (13)
Daventry William Parker School

TEENAGERS!

Teenagers hate being told anything
Except when they know it's right.
Evil to people and
Naughty at school.
Accidentally run up the phone bill.
Good sometimes.
Eat until they can't go on.
Really stroppy at times.
Spend too much money.

Louise Hunter (13)
Daventry William Parker School

ONE MAN'S LIFE

I once met a man,
He was very thick,
He worked in a place making glue sticks.

He had a daughter,
She was called Maureen,
She drank a large bottle of chlorine.

He had a wife,
She was lazy,
She was so boring she drove people crazy.

He had a dog,
He was called Mickey,
When he licks you he makes you damp and sticky!

Georgia Berry (11)
Daventry William Parker School

THE DEAD FIRE STATION

In the cellar the mouse squeaks,
Upstairs the floorboards creak,

The dead musty showers that don't work at all,
The draught that sweeps through the hall,

All they hear is the call, they sweep down the
pole at that instant call,

The fire station so fragile and empty that even if a
pin drops, a brick will fall.

Leanne Melhuish (12)
Daventry William Parker School

THOUGHTS BEFORE THE WAR

They sent a letter to a man,
Who drove a grocery van.

Calling him up to go to war,
What for?

They told him to report for training,
So England's side would be gaining.

More men to fight to win the war,
What for?

To lame, to maim, to kill another,
Someone else with a wife and mother.

They tell him it's to win the war,
What for?

Lindsay Bradley (13)
Daventry William Parker School

MY BEST FRIEND

I moved to a different school,
Where I was the only one standing
                                out in a crowd.
Then there was this girl who said 'Hi,'
She had long brown hair and light blue eyes.
For the next three months, we became best friends
But then Alison had to move away, but the
Worst thing was her mum died and that's why
                                she moved.
Her dad wanted a fresh start, we write but
it's not the same being someone else's best friend.

Simone Joyce (13)
Daventry William Parker School

BLUE

Blue is the colour of the sky,
Blue is the colour of the sea.
Blue is the colour of a key-ring,
Blue is the colour of a ping-pong ball.

Blue is a warm colour,
Blue can be light or dark.
Blue can make you happy or sad,
Blue can make you feel safe.

Blue is a wonderful colour
What would we do without it.

Blue.

Laura Sanders (12)
Daventry William Parker School

FISH IN THE SEA

Multicoloured fish flashing by,
by the sharp rocks on sea bed.
The smell of salty water.
With large round eyes,
and flapping fish,
watch the fish swim by.
And the waves splashing up
on the sandy beach.
With the green seaweed
floating on the bottom
of the ocean bed.

Laurie Shepherd (12)
Daventry William Parker School

RACE DAY

Start of the race, everyone's ready to go.
People cheering.
The bikes rev their engines.
There's my favourite number 4 soon number 2.
It's Carl, Carl Fogerty.
He is everyone's favourite.
Now they're off skidding round the corner,
Their knees dragging along the ground.
It's starting to rain.
Pit men are calling out the numbers.
They need to come in for a pair of wets.
He's done a good pit stop.
He's out in 1.5 seconds.
He comes out of the pits into second place.
Witton's first and he needs to come in for a pair of wets.
He goes in for a pit stop, he takes 11.1 seconds.
That puts Fogerty into first.
Last lap and Fogerty's going to win.
Fogerty wins.
He does a wheely over the line.
The crowd are shouting with delight.

Calvin Jones (12)
Daventry William Parker School

THE GREY KITTEN

Little grey kitten sitting there alone,
Wanting someone to take him home.
Little grey kitten sweet and innocent,
Until the door is closed.

Little grey kitten wrestling with the washing,
Little grey kitten dozing around.
Little grey kitten falls asleep,
Cuddled up in a ball.

Little grey kitten eating its food,
Little grey kitten without any name.
Little grey kitten what shall we call you,
Sooty, Sweep or Misty?

Little grey kitten you shall be called,
Misty, just like the colour you are.
Little grey kitten go to sleep,
Until dawn is here.

Kelly Muckelberg (13)
Daventry William Parker School

EVERY LITTLE BOY'S A DREAMER

I wish I could be a footballer,
Just like Ryan Giggs.
What if I end up as a farmer,
With a farm full of pigs.

When it comes to football, I'm no good,
Not as good as the other boys, not as good as I should.

I try to tackle,
It's just like a race,
When I try to score a goal,
I fall on my face.

I've never scored a goal,
I always land in mud,
I always get hurt because I land with a thud.

They always say 'You need a bath'
I start to pray but they just laugh.

It upsets me, it's just not fair!
Please help me God, if you're up there.

Stacey Pfadenhauer (11)
Daventry William Parker School

TIME TO DIE

Goodbye cruel world, farewell,
I'll see you in heaven, or would it be hell.
I can't take any more of this nightmare,
And you didn't seem to care.
How shall I die, you know I have to,
I'll use a knife, or drown in the loo.
So goodbye mum and farewell dad,
I'm going now so don't be sad.
The bully might laugh, I don't know his name,
He's in the sixth form, he's not very tame.
The unexplained bruises, the grazes, the cuts,
And now I can't take it, it's got too much.
Farewell whoever finds this note,
Your son *Steven.*

Steven Payne (13)
Daventry William Parker School

SUMMER'S OVER

Today I walked out into the garden,
Golden leaves crisp and brown.
Crunch, crunch, as I walked along the path,
I brushed my hand along the tree,
About a dozen leaves fell to the ground.
I walked some more,
The summer flowers were gone.
I drifted a little more,
The conkers fell to the ground.
And now I know that summer's over,
And winter's on its way.

Natalie Briggs (11)
Daventry William Parker School

SPACE MOUNTAIN

I sat in the seat of space mountain,
then the bars came down.
I held on very tight to my dad,
all of a sudden the ride started,
it jolted,
then stopped.
In front of me steam came flowing into our faces.
I was filled with fear.
The steam got thicker,
suddenly the ride shot up in the air,
at the speed of a rocket going into space.
Glowing planets in the darkness.
Climbing high and dipping low.
Slowly it came to a halt.

Anna Hickman (11)
Daventry William Parker School

SPORTS DAY

When it's sports day, I always pray,
that I don't end up in the sack race,
because what if I fall on my face.
When it's sports day, I always pray,
that I don't end up in the skipping race,
because there isn't much hope because I can't cope
with a big, I mean huge skipping rope.
When it's sports day, I always pray,
that I don't end up playing basketball,
because the other team are really tall,
and I don't think it's fair at all.
When it's the end of sports day, I go for a run,
in the boiling hot sun, because I got beaten by everyone.

Vikki Macefield (11)
Daventry William Parker School

THE LETTER

What is the point of war and hate?
I think it is a big mistake.
I do not see the reason why,
So many people have to die.

Guns and fires all around,
Lots of people on the ground.
Every soldier, a mother's son,
Going to war with his gun.

Each dawn arrives with another shot,
The blood on the floor marks the spot.
Hoping it will all soon end,
Lying there with his friend.

A half-written letter in his pocket,
Brought to an end by the enemy's rocket.
For him the peace arrives too late;
What is the point of war and hate?

Carmel Street (13)
Daventry William Parker School

WAR!

Massacred they are,
Hundreds at a time.
A line of men falling,
To the sound of a machine gun whirling around.

There always seems to be one going on,
Two sides disagreeing.
But what about the people fleeing,
No one listens to *their* disagreeing.

You're fighting for your freedom,
Shooting all day,
Shooting all night.
But war is not at all right.

War is a way of death,
It's not fair,
It's not right.
War.

Steven Higgins (13)
Daventry William Parker School

THE SKIER

The skier wakes up in the silent early morning.
Getting ready, he's quiet as can be.
Out he goes and gets his boots and skis.
Down to the chair-lift in the fresh, powdery, glistening snow.
When he gets there,
There's a clank, clank as the chair-lift goes round.
He gets on and goes up and up and up.
Over the tree, sparkling snow shines.
At the top he skis off into the piste.
He starts to ski on the soft, soft snow,
Zooming down towards the bottom,
Parallel turns every second,
Adrenaline is flowing fast through his body.
Then it's an even steeper drop,
It's literally vertical,
So he starts to ski down,
In and out the trees zooming down,
Until after all the adrenaline flowing slows down.
He's at the bottom,
So he goes up and up and up once again.

Neil Johnson (11)
Daventry William Parker School

WAR - FEARED SOULS

Lives wrecked,
Some old, some young.
People praying - trying to find hope.
Children's faces, covered in fear.
Soldiers hurt - they need someone near.

People hiding,
Holding each other tight,
Wondering who will survive the night.
Bombs blowing up, howl and then,
Shrapnel flying - it's happening again.
Women screaming, feeling tired,
Another bomb's blown up . . .
Another gun's been fired.

Sian Hardie (13)
Daventry William Parker School

THE GHOST

Cold air tingling around my face,
My cheeks a rosy pink.
The sky turning to deathly black.
Wind howling making my curtains fly out.
Hiding under my bed covers often taking a peep
Into the horror room.
I sit up, peer out of the window to see a
Withered old lady slithering across the lawn.
I stand staring, my eyes popping out of my head.
Slowly, steadily she fades away.

Samantha Barnes (11)
Daventry William Parker School

DARK CLOUDS

Dark clouds forming up ahead,
The blackness strikes fear in my heart.
A clap of terrifying thunder, a flash of white lightning,
I want to hide.
I quiver behind the sofa,
Or under the stairs. I want to lock myself in
Never go out.
It's dark and gloomy.
A bang! The electricity goes off.
What am I going to do?
The walls are coming in around me.
Ahhh!

Elliott Prince (11)
Daventry William Parker School

HE'S OUR RABBIT

With big beady eyes,
hating being handled,
he curls up into a fat fur ball.
Ears bound together like scissors,
with big chunks bitten out of them.
He snatches bits of food,
as he bashes his bowl around.
His nails are as sharp as knives.
Stuck inside a cage and run it's as if he's in jail.
Intensely waiting for freedom.
He's our rabbit!

Chris Osborne (11)
Daventry William Parker School

OLD DOG

'Goodbye' old dog,
I will never see you again.
Your food bowl, now always will remain empty,
Your last drops of remaining water are still in your water bowl.
A few old chewed up toys lay lifeless on the lawn,
The old mud-stained football stands in a huge puddle.
I whistle for you but you don't come,
Your lead hangs on the peg as usual.
It is time for your food but you're not there,
It's time to take you for your walk, you're not there.
You're never going to be there,
Never again!
'Goodbye' old dog,
See you next time my faithful friend.

Andrew Payne (13)
Daventry William Parker School

THE CAT

Coloured as the black of night,
It slips through the open gap.
Around the garden it prowls,
Green eyes gleaming.
To the fence it crawls,
Springing to the top.
Sharp claws clench the wood,
As it hauls up its slender shape.
On its journey it slides,
Into the night.

Katie Megan Sales (11)
Daventry William Parker School

THE NIGHT CREEPER

At night it sneaks around the house,
Without a sound or a murmur.
It slithers past my door,
Waiting, waiting.
I hear it breathe within my room,
It could be under my bed,
It could be by my door.
When I tell my mum and dad,
They say I must have dreamt it.
I know it's in our house,
I know it.
I can smell it,
A disgusting smell fills the house,
Like fumes fill a factory.
I've never seen it or heard it move,
But I know it's there.
I know it.

Karen Baguley (13)
Daventry William Parker School

AUTUMN DAYS

The crispy golden leaves fall off to the ground,
The ripe conkers ready to be found.
The tops of the trees start to get bare,
Mother Nature changes with great care.
As the days get shorter and colder,
Our shadows grew longer and longer.
As the autumn wind goes cold,
Then the winter unfolds.

Daniel Lee (11)
Daventry William Parker School

AT THE SEASIDE

Crashing down and up the rocks,
Come the waves.
Sparkling sand glistens in the
Sun.
Children making sandcastles with
Buckets and spades.
Then the sea goes calm and then
calmer at night.
Blues and greens being mixed up
In the sea.
All the different animals spread
in the sea.
I hope everybody has a good time
at the seaside.

Samantha Beames (11)
Daventry William Parker School

GOAL

The ball shoots over his head,
It soars through the air like a bird,
And hits the back of the net.
The crowd roars.
30,000 lions jumping up and down.
Derby fans are sitting down, depressed,
The goalie stands there,
Totally helpless,
He let it in,
He let us score.

Katherine Smithson (11)
Daventry William Parker School

CRIES OF WAR

Blue blood, cries of wounds,
Children scream, cry and wail.
Bombs drop, guns fire.
Screams of terror,
Scared to go outside.
No peace, no quiet,
Cries of babies.
Explosions, buildings crumpled.
Everywhere's a mess,
Everything's burning.
All ablaze,
Silence strikes,
It's over.

Hayley Rogers (11)
Daventry William Parker School

WAR

Hundreds killed, thousands injured.
When peace fails and war breaks out,
Friends and relatives say goodbye,
To the soldiers in the army.
Crying as they leave,
Not certain whether they will come back
Alive and living well.
So anxious for months and years.
Praying they'll come back with only a cut or bruise,
But they know well this is not true.
Because this is the start of the First World War.
They do not know there are many more to come,
With hundreds killed and thousands injured.

Emma Hummerston (13)
Daventry William Parker School

WAR!

War is black,
Nobody's right.
Lots of death,
Without a fight.

Guns that kill,
Bombs that maim.
Hospitals full,
Without any name.

Generals that shout,
At father and son.
Bullets that fly,
But nowhere to run.

Planes that bomb,
Rockets that explode.
Lorries full of soldiers,
That fill the road.

War is sudden,
War is loud.
Nobody wins,
No one's proud.

Aaron Shepherd (13)
Daventry William Parker School

THE TEARS OF A CLOWN

I sit and wonder why I'm here,
Or where I'm going to.
I feel encaged like a deer,
My home is like a zoo.

The people look and laugh at me,
With my goofy clothes.
They don't understand how I feel,
The tears aren't just for show.

My big red nose and purple hair,
My shoes are size 19.
I run around the circus floor,
My ears are bright and green!

I want to find a real life,
I want to be a norm.
Not to have pies in my face,
Would put me back on form.

My heart sinks when people ask:
'So what's your living? What do you do?'
I tell them, then they laugh,
I wish it was not true.

So when you see another clown,
Don't mock or play a joke.
For beneath the paint and fuzzy hair,
Is a normal kind of bloke.

Kim Bates (13)
Daventry William Parker School

A WAR POEM

War, a word that causes such pain,
Something which affects many people.
Dead massacred bodies lying in the drain,
Things you cannot ignore no matter how hard you try.
Letting friends and relations go to war,
Worrying about them night and day.
Their choice to go to battle in anger,
You worry how hard they'll pay.

The influence of leaders over others,
Knowing you'll have to do what they say.
Realising you could be killing your brothers,
Going out on auto-pilot and just mowing down anyone.

Sitting in a muddy trench, contemplating the future,
The fear of death, being blown up or shot.
Being injured and sent home,
In disgrace, in poverty, without a lot.

From the disgusting conditions hearing a groan of pain,
Knowing it could have been a comrade,
One that only lived down the lane.
You're all in the same situations, sharing powerful emotions.

Laura Skelcey (13)
Daventry William Parker School

SNAIL SPORTS

Last night on my garden wall,
Two snails were having a game of football.
They passed the ball around the tree,
The final score was 4 - 3.
Then they went in their shell,
Which is where all snails dwell.

Last night in the thicket,
Two snails were playing cricket.
The tortoises were messing about,
Because they were already out.
The snails went in their shell,
Which is where all snails dwell.

Melanie Newton (11)
Daventry William Parker School

LITTLE BROTHERS

Little brothers can be such a pain,
I'm sure making you angry is their only aim.

They can really drive you up the wall,
And almost make you want to call . . .
'My little brother is such a pain,
I wish he'd go away and not come back again!'

I agree that some are cuddly and cute,
But judging by mine these cases are fairly minute.
I can give you examples of why they're so bad,
For those that think I'm exaggerating by just a tad.

There's the time that he covered my homework with egg,
And at break when he wouldn't let go of my leg.
Oh, and then there's the time at the Christmas play,
Where he tripped over the donkey in such a way,
That he went head over heels through the stable door,
And squashed baby Jesus all over the floor!

My friends didn't speak to me for the rest of the week,
And when they did it was as though I was a geek.
Now that you've seen what little brothers are like,
If your mum's having one I suggest you get on your bike!

Mark Odell (12)
Daventry William Parker School

LOVE AND HATE

I love my family
And I love my dog.
I love Sunday dinners,
And I love my big bed.

I like football, rugby
And basketball.
I like going on holidays
And I like being told I'm a good boy.

I *don't* like Coronation Street,
Home and Away or Neighbours.
I *don't* like homework.
And I *don't* like girlie games.

I hate school,
Girls,
Jeans and
Fruit.

Charley Fagan (11)
Daventry William Parker School

A MORNING AT THE DENTIST

Pull it out, pull it out,
It hurts too much.
Pull it out, pull it out,
It hurts at the touch.

I could have been playing football,
Instead I'm here wasting my time.
I'm sitting here in agony,
Oh, it's such a crime.

I could have even been playing rugby,
With all that running about,
I'm pretty sure it could have been
easily knocked out.

Oh bliss, at last, free of pain,
But I can't play football or rugby because
It's pouring down with rain.

Benjamin Murrell (11)
Daventry William Parker School

THE POISONED TREE

The empty skies echoed,
Despite the evening air.
It climbed up the wall,
And despair fell as time went to fall.

The chain dug deep,
The tree screamed
With pain, despair and disbelief.

The tree was poisoned.
A bird flew down,
It got caught in its spooky grip.
It tried to get free,
It was enclosed forever.

The snow fell gently on the stone-hearted tree.
It stood there and gazed at the house.
The bird fell and the tree came crashing down
Around the bird's body,
Leaving a space around where it lay,
To its death.

Hannah Morrice (13)
Daventry William Parker School

LOVE

Emotional kisses.
A scent of love.
Warm, soft, the hands of affection.
Glorious heaven fills my mind.
Tender, loving care.
Arms hold tight, a deadly dream starts through the night.
No warmth and no more kisses.
Stolen from your friend.
Heartbroken, lonely, cold.
Emotional kisses, but not to me.
The scent of love flows away.
Lost to her like no meaning, no life.
Cold tears running, but happiness to them.
Lost my lover to my best friend.
Empty room I sit alone, crying in the dark.
Sad and lost without him who no one could replace.
I want him, I need him, I love him but he loved her and not me.
But I still love you.

Wendy Lau (13)
Daventry William Parker School

WORMS

Nobody likes me,
Everybody hates me,
Just 'cause I eat worms.
I bite their heads off,
Suck their juice out,
Throw their skins away.
You'll be surprised,
How I can survive,
On one three times a day.

Gavin Binder (11)
Daventry William Parker School

NOTHING

Nothing creeps through the house,
Nothing stalks the streets.
Nothing walks the town at night,
Nothing is nothing.
Nothing has no name,
Nothing has no smell.
Nothing is nothing.
You can't see nothing,
You can't hear nothing,
And you can't smell nothing.
But nothing is there somewhere,
So what is nothing?
Is it something or nothing?
Well I know one thing,
Nothing means nothing but nothing
To me.

Rebekah Sharpe (13)
Daventry William Parker School

FISHING

F reezing cold early mornings,
I cy, cold, dark and damp.
S etting up my line and tackle,
H urling ground-bait through the mist.
I nto my chair, curling up, keeping warm,
N odding off, it's so very early.
G rumbling at the ducks eating my bait.

David Giles (11)
Daventry William Parker School

GOODBYE BEST FRIEND

Standing there with tears rolling out of my eyes,
Staring at the beautiful flowers which lie there.
And feeling empty and sad inside,
Wanting that to be me, not her.
Thinking how my life would be without her around,
While still trying to get over the shock.
Now my eyes explode with tears,
My life's just not worth living.
Why?
Why did it have to be her?
Why couldn't it have been me?
There she goes deep down underground,
And then up to heaven.
Goodbye best friend,
Goodbye.

Amanda Haynes (13)
Daventry William Parker School

SWIMMING

S wimming gives you exercise,
W hile having fun as well.
I   t makes you feel good inside,
M en, women and children will all love it.
M e, myself, I love swimming,
I   t fills me with fun and pleasure.
N obody I know dislikes swimming.
G oing for a swim makes me feel happy.

Victoria Thompson (12)
Daventry William Parker School

MY FOOTBALL TEAM

Bournemouth are the best,
Because they've passed the test.
They've passed the test of skill,
But had to pay the bill.

A small club like they are,
Who want to go real far,
Must hold the purse strings tight,
And play with all their might.

In last year's title race,
They almost lost their place.
When debts kept going up,
And they went out the cup.

Although they nearly sank,
They were rescued from the bank.
Now fans, they own the club,
And support it with much love.

I've seen 15 matches,
With lots of goalie catches.
And players who all shoot,
With head or either boot.

Bournemouth I love you,
And so does my family too.
I went through a lot of tears,
But I'll support you all my years.

James Topp (11)
Daventry William Parker School

My Own Alliteration Poem

Take two wicked witches,
Seven evil eyes.
Nine man-eating rats,
Sixteen bouncing brains.
Twenty-one scary skeletons,
One messy monster.
Four silly fish,
Three screams of laughter.
One million ghastly ghosts,
A thousand slithery snakes,
And fifty-one vile vampire bats.

Alliteration

Selina Bishop (11)
Daventry William Parker School

The Mind Of The Machine

The labyrinth of boilers,
There it is again, coming closer,
In the back of my mind the rigid scraping.
The steam is wafting towards me,
There it is the battered fedora hat,
Swiftly moving towards me,
No mercy, no love only hate inside the mind of the machine.
I feel myself run,
But the fire-hot breath is always on my neck.
The mind of the machine.

Matthew Elder (13)
Daventry William Parker School

PAUL

She shivered,
It's cold.
What was that?
Oh, just the cat.
She climbed into bed,
She had seen something out of the corner of her eye.
Paul?
No, Paul's dead.
She heard a baby cry.
Paul. It is you.
She ran across the landing and into the nursery,
She looked down at the cradle, there was no one there.
It was true.
Paul is dead.
My little baby.
My flesh and blood. Dead.
Why did he die?
Was it my fault?
Yes, it is.
It's my fault. I'll never see him again.
It's my fault he lost his life.
He probably would have lived to 90 if it wasn't for me.

Francesca McEwen (13)
Daventry William Parker School

WE ALL STAND ALONE

We all stand alone.
The house is not a place,
It's a fear.
As we walk closer,
The wind warns us away.
But we can't listen.
The doors invite us in.
In a trance we walk through,
Invisible hands pulling us in.
The dark surrounds us,
It suffocates us.
The stairs fall down to us,
And we begin to climb.
Someone slips, someone falls,
Where, we don't know.
The top of the stairs,
Reaches out to us.
And blindly we carry on.
No one speaks,
No one dares.
The silence chills us.
One of us runs,
Their footsteps make no sound.
Hardly anyone left.
A door, the door is open.
I step through.
Someone screams.
They run away.
I am all alone.

Sara Fawcett (13)
Daventry William Parker School

HEBRIDES

My dad's birth place, my gran's resting place.
Vast flat land, with miserable weather.
The wind pounds against my red cheeks.
The powerful wind draws the tears from my eyes with great force.
The rugged coast like jaws that have taken many a life.
As the day ends the boats slowly move in
And the seamen come and weigh their fish.
The sun drops and the seals rise. In a frenzy of calling.
Many a pleasant dream!

Tim Innocent (13)
Daventry William Parker School

AUTUMN

Chocolate, caramel and cream,
Turns the colour of the leaves.
The cold comes in,
And the warm goes out.
Autumn is in people's minds.
As a cold and misty,
Time of year.

Sian Powell (11)
Daventry William Parker School

THE WAVE

He whispers my name,
Calling me to dance with him.
His voice rings out clear,
Hollow,

And yet so full of life.

His arms reach out,
Beckoning me towards him,
And his cool fingers,
Entwine with mine,

As we move as one.

I become hypnotised,
By his swirling movements,
And I get drawn further,
Into his deep blue eyes.

I look nowhere else,
Except at him,

I see nothing around me,

Hear nothing.

His wild hair,
White as snow,
Whips back sharply
In the cold breeze.

It contacts my face,
Causing me to slip,
And loose my footing,
On the unseen floor below.
As I regain my balance,
And turn once more to face him,
He is no longer there.

He has gone.

Emily Carter (17)
Duston Upper School

UPSET

You've got to pick your time:
Allow the sentiment to be missed,
Let the feel die and turn,
You'll bruise so much more easily,
If you're quiet.
If you wait for the blink,
The catch of time to arrive:
Safe, warm and happy.

You'll bleed so much more easily,
If you're mannered and restrained.
If you don't let them see,
The mess and mess
You've become.
You bleed,
Only on yourself,
And hope they notice the stains.

David Moore (17)
Duston Upper School

HOLD MY HAND

A bomb, a gun,
A daughter, a son.
Innocence, guilt,
Courage rebuilt.
Scared, alive,
Must survive.
Trauma, pain,
I'm not to blame.
Don't understand,
Hold my hand.
Don't want to stay,
Get me away.
Take me home,
Where I'm not alone.

Maria Walding (18)
Duston Upper School

JEALOUSY

A spitting fire
Of evil works,
Hatred twanging
Like a bow string.
Frost that has eaten
Away the joyful summer.
A pain from
Deep inside your soul,
Jealousy.

Mocking sun,
Burning through
Bullets of rain.
A hungry sea,
Lapping up betrayal.
Tall trees whispering,
Dark secrets thither.
An icy web
Of misunderstanding.
Jealousy.

Beware!

Elizabeth Whitaker (12)
Kingsthorpe Middle School

ODE TO A SHOE-LACE

Oh magnificent shoe-lace
where would I be without you?
Oh, what on earth would I do?
You come in such a conglomeration of colours.
I love your sleek, slender shape
And the way you're so magnificent
with your impeccable plastic ends.
I adore the way you so willingly keep
my shoes done up so splendidly.
You're irreplaceable, priceless and unique.
You have so many amazing uses
you do so many exceptional things
such as hold my hair back so miraculously
or superbly support my champion conker.
And the way you're always there for
me whenever I'm in a crisis.
When you cunningly hold up my knickers
when the elastic embarrassingly snaps.
When I'm despairing for a necklace you
come to my rescue and look sensational
when adorned with dazzling gems.
You safely secure precious, priceless
papers and keep bundled together
neglected, tattered newspapers.
Oh shoe-lace you are everything to me
Without you I am dissatisfied
So please don't ever break or snap
For a broken shoe-lace means a
broken heart.

Shelly Smith (13)
Millway Middle School

ODE TO MY KETTLE

Oh wonderful, marvellous kettle,
How you willingly boil all day!
With your bottle-green exterior,
What more can I possibly say?
I value the way you switch off
When your job is done,
And the bubbling, fizzing sound that you make
No one can mistake.
When you're boiling, I know
For the steam tells me so
And the mug with the milk lies waiting.
You're brilliant, you're fantastic
You make a fabulous cup of tea
Oh, how magnificent you are to any family.
When I'm ill, you help me get better
When I'm cold, you make me warm
Never have you complained that you feel worn.
Whether night or late morning
Afternoon or when it's dawning
You'll gladly be switched on
You're my only number one.
How sensational you are
Oh, glamorous and adorable
Kettle.

Caroline Benson (12)
Millway Middle School

CAR

Ode to our beautiful car,
You are so wonderful in every way,
You speed along endless motorways,
You slide gracefully down busy main roads
You're sleek, shiny extravagant,
And the cute little numbers
on your back and front,
They are so radical and so unique to
you and only you.
You drive us everywhere,
no matter how near or far,
You are a member of our family,
You are our everlasting friend,
You make our lives so much easier,
Your revving and astounding engine never fails,
The glamorous '*beep*' is music to our ears,
The amazing and staggering sound
of your indicators,
Sends a shiver down my spine,
Your amazing soft seats,
makes endless journeys seem,
So comfortable and relaxed,
Your wheels are so smooth and steady,
Like satin material,
Oh, marvellous car
We couldn't live without you,
But please next time,
Pay for your own petrol!

Chloe Mulholland (12)
Millway Middle School

AN ODE TO MY WATCH

Oh, my glorious watch, I need you so,
You tell me the time of day,
When you strike, my heart stops still.
Your face, so sleek to kill,
You were discovered just for me, of course.
When you stop, you don't cry out in pain.
I rest a battery in your back, you start ticking
once again.
Your slender strap curls round my wrist,
The buckle is silver, chrome, delightful.
The tartan pattern on your strap blends carefully
together in harmony as in a choir.
You are unique, an individual, should I say.
If I lose you, my world is lost.
I can rely on you when I want to know the time,
How do you cope with the stress of ticking and
moving, ticking and moving?
Your curved, bubble-lettered numbers carefully
placed around your face,
This makes it easier for me to perceive,
When a clock doesn't work, I have trust in you.
You educate me to tell the time of day,
You're so important, more than you could ever know.
I think you're the world, we are the perfect match
I'll be infatuated with you, till I'm old and grey.
I unbuckle you from around my wrist,
Just for the night, goodnight watch, I'll see you in
the morning light.
No more reflections on your beautiful face.
I now say goodnight again.

Martine Landeman (12)
Millway Middle School

ODE TO MY HAIRBRUSH

Hairbrush, oh hairbrush I love you
  so much
The way you slide, purposefully down
  my back and leave bright red streaks
  on my neck
You go everywhere with me you always
  will
We're together, forever we're stuck like
  glue
Your chewed white handle will not
  depart from my hand
Your genuine Denman mark makes you
  so grand
You're my lethal weapon better than
  a sword
Your slender white figure brings joy
  to behold.
Hairbrush, oh hairbrush I love you so
  much
I treasure, I cherish every moment
  we touch.

Debbie Asplin (13)
Millway Middle School

ODE TO A COOKER

Oh you wonderful, marvellous cooker
What would I do without you?
You cook my food every hour of the day
But your complaints are extremely few.

You're sensational, spectacular
Fantastic and miraculous
The way you cook any food, any kind
Is Absolutely Fabulous.

You are always there when I need you
It doesn't matter if it's day or night
Your delicious, mouth-watering meals
Make any dull day bright.

The pans used to cook your brilliant food
Are hardly ever on the shelf
But if you can cook tasty meals
Why can't you clean yourself?

Sarah Griffey (12)
Millway Middle School

AN ODE TO A PAPER CLIP

Oh paper clip, oh paper clip
With your slender, shiny arcs
And your wonderfully slightly bowed straights
You so elegantly hold together my work
You're more ingenious than a staple any day
You possess nothing, you're courteous,
Yet you never complain.
You're in tremendous condition,
With your vibrant plastic cocoon
And your extravagant sharp ends
You're compulsory for my organisation
You're convenient to use and you co-operate
brilliantly
Some think you're pointless but I think
you're superb.
You bring a starry light to my life
You fulfil your function completely
I'd nominate you for every award possible
But you have a single, unfortunate problem
Why can I never find you when I need you?

Amanda Hampson (12)
Millway Middle School

PEN

Oh cartridge pen oh cartridge pen
Your splendid colours shine
Red, yellow and green they are
They do shine so very fine
Your sophisticated ink that slithers across the page,
Never feeling selfish and not wanting to write,
Instead you are always so merciful,
The only time you let me down is when that ink has
disappeared,
You rest in my hand so steady and upright,
I hold you so tightly when you write,
You are my pride and joy in every possible way,
Your performance in writing is always so phenomenal
I admire your silver tip that sparkles with the shine of
the sun,
Your beauty is incredible,
You have made me write more fluently,
And your loyalty to me is everlasting.

Rachael Clarkson (12)
Millway Middle School

ODE TO MY MICROWAVE

Oh microwave, wonderful microwave
You are a marvellous machine
I could not survive without you
I love the way you make mouth-watering
Meals in just three minutes.
You are my joy
You are my God
I worship you, microwave
I love the way you get hot without
complaining.
You cook nearly everything under the sun
You even defrost.
You are a phenomenal, wondrous,
miraculous machine.
You are my only desire
If you go I would not exist
Not even for a day.
I use you nearly every time I need a little snack.
I switch you on, set the timer and wait
For you to triumphantly shout . . . *'Ping'!*

Andrea Byrne (12)
Millway Middle School

WINTER

As winter comes all the days get shorter,
Then the dawn does not arrive as quickly;
The cold temperatures are like torture,
With the trees bare, the branches are prickly
After days become very dark and grey,
And snowflakes begin to float from the sky;
Then the ground turns silver during the day,
With numbers of snowmen getting quite high;
The cold weather is then put on the run,
All the snow then begins to disappear;
All of this happens because of the sun,
After spring begins to get very near;
      With the days slowly becoming longer,
      Winter's long reign of the earth is over.

Oliver Newton (12)
Millway Middle School

NOVEMBER

November makes me think of leaves
    falling off the trees.
On firework day it can be very
    pretty in the night.
Very dark and cold in the night
    and very wet too.
Early in the morning I would rather
    stay in bed.
Making a hole in a conker makes
    me feel happy.
Bit of soup I like to eat when I
    am very cold.
Early in the morning we have to
    get dressed up warm.
Remembrance day is a time when we
    remember the people in the war.

Laura Brown (9)
Newton Road Junior School

THE SPELLBOUND WITCH

The cauldron boils with witch's brew
Not the normal English stew
The witch throws in all kinds of things
Like the eyes of newts and even wasp stings
She wonders to whom this spell she will feed
While she mixes it with a lily pond reed.
Then without any warning the brew explodes
And turns the witch into an ugly old toad
There's nothing she can do she's in great pain
And since then she's never been seen again.

Angela Yussuff (11)
Northampton High School

POWER

Power is something many people hold over me.
My parents, my conscience and my teachers.
Power is the surge of the sea
and the strength of love between my family.

My teachers have power
but in a different way,
if they told me to do something
I would do it no doubt straightaway.

I have power over my sister
but she often does not do what I say.
She would listen if it was my mother
or my father.
They are really the only people she listens to,
well she is only three.

Everybody has powerful people who tell them what
to do.
Parents and bosses have one too.
But the greatest power of all is love.

Katy Blane (11)
Northampton High School

THE MIXTURE

One night I was out upon my broom,
Flying over the rooftops: zoom, zoom!
The wind was blowing in my face so cold,
I was beginning to feel much more bold.

Now to make that magic mixture,
To put all to sleep who take,
Just a drop of the evil medicine,
Then never ever to wake.

The odd and rare ingredients,
For this most awful of my spells,
Collected from the woods at midnight,
To be sure to work very well.

The potion now ready for whoever,
Deserves to go fast asleep,
Only to wake when I say so,
From a sleep that is so deep.

Kate Greenhalgh (11)
Northampton High School

THE BIGGEST SPELL OF ALL

I need a newt's tongue,
A bullet from a gun,
A dash of princess' hair,
And a touch of breath air,
For the biggest spell of all.

I will need a spoon,
So my spell will be turned,
No lips to tell,
My magic spell,
For the biggest spell of all.

A human ear,
So that my spell can hear,
The magic words I chant.
Frumpty, frump, bumpty bump,
I call the spirits from their beds
For the biggest spell of all.

Rebecca Ribbans (12)
Northampton High School

HAVE YOU EVER MET A WITCH?

Have you ever met a witch,
Strolling down the street?
They stare at you,
With hungry eyes,
Like a dog that craves fresh meat.

Have you ever met a witch,
Walking to the shop?
Beware, beware,
Take no need,
If she offers you soda-pop!

Have you ever met a witch,
Down by the old farm track?
She's dressed to the nines,
In her smartest rags,
Which are coloured . . . all in black?

Have you ever met a witch,
Behind you in a queue?
And you wonder,
As you look at her,
Is she after you?

Antonia Stewart (11)
Northampton High School

POWER

Power is a witch's spell
A wizard's wand,
A sorcerer's potion.
Power is the hurricane
The volcano
Or the flood
Power is in Miss Cramp's stare
A moody teacher's glare
Or a mad teacher's temper beginning
to flare.
Power is a laser beam
A bow or arrow
A shooting bullet
Power is in the Queen's fine speech
In God's flash of light
In the government's parliament seat.
But power is in little things like
a sudden brain-wave
A battery's short life
Or a piece of strange music.
Power is everywhere
Somewhere we want it
And somewhere we don't.

Joanne Ayris (11)
Northampton High School

A Spell To Turn A Frog Into A Black Cat

Black bat wings,
A fair maiden's rings,
A spiky thistle
One toothbrush bristle;

Eye of snake,
A weed from a lake,
One slimy snail,
A banshee's wail;

The highest apple from a tree,
A drop of salt from the sea,
A pint of water from a well,
Will give a most revolting smell.

One large bullfrog,
A wart from a hog,
Into the pot and boil it well,
To finish off my black cat spell.

Gemma Pirnie (11)
Northampton High School

Spellbound

One final cackle, then it's done
Another day is dead, and gone.
With the slam of a door
Up, up with a soar.

Over churchyards she did fly,
Scrawling on a moonless sky.
She saw a sexton down below,
Digging with a twisted hoe.

Her spindly frame, wrapped round the broom
Engulfed with a sense of chilling doom.
Birds shot quickly out of view,
To let the evil woman through.

The black cavern welcomed her in,
Wretched smells came from within,
There was an eerie sense of people there,
No one could however be seen there.

Katharine Clark (14)
Northampton High School

A WITCH?

My brother and I were once walking by,
A strange little house with a woman nearby,
She muttered these words and flew away,
Just in case we decided to stay.

Humble tumble roll and fun,
I see a person on the run,
She flew on a broomstick high in the sky,
We were puzzled that a woman could fly.

Not long after the door creaked open,
A kind lady let us in,
She told us about ugly Winnie the wicked witch,
And mentioned her peculiar itch,

She's not too bad you must understand,
She's really my cousin from a faraway land!

Zoe Corbishley (11)
Northampton High School

A FULL MOON CHANT

Heat a cauldron on the hearth,
Add two newts and a bat's heart.

Now for a witch's favourite drink,
Slimy thick green ink.

Mix crushed frogs' legs with spiders' webs,
A bowl of mouldy jelly and a farmer's
Dog's chewed welly.

Put in the screams of a rollercoaster ride,
And a snake that's three metres wide.

Stir with a rusty spoon,
And leave the rest to the moon.

Sarah Jennings (12)
Northampton High School

WITCH MACOY'S RECIPE

Four bats' eyes and frogs' legs,
Some lizards, snakes too.
Blind mice and rats' tails,
I'm looking for you!

Now some cats' brains,
Don't forget the snails.
Teachers are scrumptious
As well as toe nails!

In goes a tarantula,
Complete with its brains.
Now my spell is ready,
Here it goes again!

Charlotte Crosby (11)
Northampton High School

... AND FINALLY A NICE PLUMP FRESH TOAD

My fellow toads have asked me to say,
That menus with toads have had their day.
We need new recipes, exciting spells,
A cookery book that really sells.

Toads are warty, leathery creatures
With rather sad, unpleasant features.
Be like Delia and cook something big;
A cow, a sheep, a duck or a pig!

And think of the veggie witches too,
They don't want toads polluting their brew.
You say toad flavour enhances your grog,
But we urge you - try something new like
... frog!

Victoria Morris (12)
Northampton High School

SPELLBOUND

Witches dance around their pot,
round their brews steaming hot
plop in this and plop in that,
eyes of newt and ears of cat,
a feather or two and a rotting egg,
slugs and snails and a spider's leg.
Day by day, night by night,
as the sun and moon shine bright
they plot and they plan,
all that they can.
Do not take a sniff, you will drop down dead.
Mind you, that is what they want it is said.

Becky Doyle (11)
Northampton High School

THE COVEN

They sat in a circle,
A fearsome sight,
Their evil eyes lit by the
Dancing fire light,

With their hunched backs,
And blackened grins,
The cackling sound,
Made a frightful din,

With a spiny hand the cauldron
Was stirred,
In went legs of a toad,
And wings of a bird,

The warlocks and witches
Were casting their spells,
And far in the distance the
Howling wolf wails,

Who dares disturb this terrible scene,
This grotesque vision that's evil and mean.

Robyn Notley (11)
Northampton High School

SPELLBOUND

The garden binds its spell
as I walk deeper within,
the silence settles like a sleepy cat,
and I feel no wish to disturb it,
and anyway, I find I cannot.

Golden green sunlight
like fabrics spread out to show
a customer its worth
over counters like bushes and lawns

The serenity and glow -
draped across the garden by quiet zephyrs;
tangled in branches;
sieved through leaves
to stencil the grass with flick'ring patterns

Tucked away corners,
bathed in silence;
like dark secrets -
always there but never acknowledged

The day dies,
and the light deepens and darkens.
The shadows take on an added menace.
But the garden has spun its spell,
and I find I cannot escape.

Katie Allen (14)
Northampton High School

SPELLBOUND

A horse's whisper. a caterpillar's length,
The butterfly's beauty and a thrush's song,
She throws them in and stirs them up.

A teacher's command, a family's love
A rose's fragrance and the noise of a crowd,
She adds some more and makes it bubble.

The smell of pine, and a touch of silk,
The joys of a baby and heat of the sun,
She tips them and the level rises.

The light of the star, the coo of a pigeon,
The hate of evil and the pain of death,
All mixed up, it froths and hisses.

The happiness of Christmas, the deepness of sleep,
Colours of the rainbow, a flash of light,
All stirred in, it's nearly ready!

The heat and cold and rage of fire,
A working child and the longing for food.
The spell has brewed and simmers gently.

Everything that has been put in her spell,
Will add to her finished creation,
The harmony of the world.

Alice Moody (12)
Northampton High School

THE WITCH'S SPELL

Heat the hob
to feed the lot.
Take the children
out their beds,
boil the cauldron,
kill them dead.

Heat the hob,
and add a frog,
a newt, a toad
and the rest,
and a rat's tail,
they're the best!

Heat the hob,
put in a blob
of bat's blood
put it in the frame,
along with a claw from a dragon's foot,
that's if you can make the claim.

Cool the hob,
you've done the job!
Just a few more steps to go!
Drink the juice,
just one more sip,
there, you've turned into a moose.

Jean Mallock (13)
Northampton High School

TRAPPED IN A SPELL

(Dedicated to my Granny, Mrs Celia Jones)

Trapped in a circle three metres wide,
Can't break the seal and there's nowhere to hide.
I push and pull but it won't give in,
I'm trapped like garbage at the bottom of the bin.

I scream and shout but no one can hear,
Where is my mum and dad, aren't they near?
It's like a bouncy castle, you fall off the side,
Then you hit the floor with your rather large hide.

Who put this round me? Who closed me in?
Is that someone's voice? Is that my best friend Lynn?
'Wait Lynn, get me out,'
But she couldn't hear me shout.

Actually she couldn't see,
So she walked on straight past me.
Then I lent upon the bars,
And suddenly I felt a jar.

Mum grabbed my arm,
'You silly old fool.
Get this jumper off,
Or else you won't go in the pool.'

Lucy Byrne (13)
Northampton High School

SPELLBOUND

What does he look like
What does he do
How tall is he
Is he looking at you?
Cupid's arrow could hit,
What would you do?
You may wonder and wonder
Has it hit him too?

What does he look like
What does he do
How tall is he
Is he looking at you?
You may not have known it,
But Cupid sure knew
You were to fall in love
With a guy he knew.

What does he look like
What does he do
How tall is he
Is he looking at you?
Are you still waiting?
You may be in the queue
But you will never know,
Until the arrow hits you!

Emma Panebianco (14)
Northampton High School

SPELLBOUND

The cool breeze whipped through my hair,
As I gulped down the moisture-laden wind.
Slowly, I took in my surroundings,
Until at last my eyes settled on the view below.
Leaves tumbled down the hill, into the stream,
Where they were swept along with the gushing flow,
And then, from beneath the dark waters,
A young seal lifted his sculptured head,
His dark eyes taking in all around him,
Before returning to his watery bed,
And then a little further along,
He raised his handsome face to the glare of the sun,
And glided elegantly through the blue waters.
Then for many minutes, I watched spellbound
As he dived and leapt and played.
Until, exhausted he returned to land,
Where he waddled silently up the sand,
And then I saw, something I had not noticed before,
For in a sheltered sandy bay, a whole colony of seals lay.
They called and shouted and yelped and screeched
From where they rested, basking in the sun.
The water lapped on the shore down below,
Where paradise is, I'll always know.

Sarah Rogers (14)
Northampton High School

SPELLBOUND

I was spellbound.
Never had the flowers talked to me before.
'She is bad,' they said. 'Evil,' said the pot plant.
'Who?' I asked.
'She talks to us,' they murmured. 'She tells us things,'
they whispered.
'Who?' I demanded.
'She feeds the birds,' they replied.

After dinner I was clearing up the dinner plates
when my mother came into the kitchen.
'Oh no!' she exclaimed. 'Do not put the leftovers
in the bin, I can feed them to the birds!'
and at that point I knew who it was,
I knew what the plants were talking about, I understood them.

The birds had stopped eating worms, they preferred the leftovers,
The worms had dramatically increased in number,
The government had to act fast.
They invented a worm-eater machine but it mechanically failed,
It went into overpower and turbo-charge.
Soon all the worm population was dead, the flowers started
to die too.
The worms were not fertilising the soil anymore and by law
fertilisers and chemicals had been banned.
The plants soon died and with them so did flower power.
I now understood what the flowers that day had prophesied,
but it was too late.
I had been too spellbound in that the flowers had actually
talked to me, and now they were dead.
My mother had managed to kill the plants.
The talking flowers.

Julie Yau (14)
Northampton High School

POWERS OF WOMEN

Never understate a woman's deception,
Her appearance is always so sweet,
But her aim in life is to destroy,
Every unsuspecting male she'll meet.

She'll engulf him in all her beauty,
The locks that surround her face,
Then she'll paralyse all of his brain cells,
And remove him without a trace.

So if you are a man with no senses,
And don't take my advice,
One woman or another,
Will ruin your entire life.

Helen Legg (14)
Northampton High School

SPELLBOUND

Who invented these difficult words
Where letters are silent and shouldn't be heard,
Where some you need one, or maybe two,
Where some seem the letters are far too few.
I start to think I've figured it out,
And then I begin to have some doubt,
I look and write, it all goes wrong
Realising it should be twice as long.
Words like mane, main and Maine,
Are really quite different but sound the same.
There are these and then there are more,
Whose meaning I've never heard before.
All they do is tangle our minds,
Why can't there be words of different kinds?

Lydia Bartram (14)
Northampton High School

SPELLBOUND

The witches looked down from the heavens above,
Casting their spells of hate, anger, love.
Controlling the people, what they say,
Allowing the people, if they may.

They see two people drifting apart,
Each one has broken the other's heart.
This was not meant to be, the witches could tell,
Another love spell they'd have to sell.

The witches muttered and mumbled their verse,
Getting some powder from out of their purse.
Throwing it down on the people they saw,
Hoping that they would need no more.

In an instant the two exchanged a look,
Silencing the hurt that they had mistook.
The anger drifted away in a second,
Rejecting the fear that once had beckoned.

Two happy customers the witches thought,
No longer were they mad and fraught.
The two walked off, hand in hand,
Over the beaches of golden sand.

The witches went back to doing what they did best,
Helping the lives of those that were messed.
Helping them out in their hour of need,
Always happy to do a good deed.

The people below are unaware,
Of the witches' never ending affair.
Sorting their lives out round after round,
Turning them into people spellbound.

Chloe Evans (14)
Northampton High School

THE WITCH'S SPELL

Hiterly, piterly, one, two, three,
wiggle your toes and come with me,
listen very carefully and do as I say,
and then I will teach you just how to play.

First you must add the flame of a dragon,
then you must add the wheel of a wagon,
secondly you must take the wings of a fairy,
and then the tooth from a girl named Mary.
Now you must add a piece of the sun,
and lastly you must load it all into a gun.

Now you must go way up high,
way up high into the sky.
Put the gun up to your eye,
pull the trigger and you will fly.

Catherine Guillaume (11)
Northampton High School

AT A PEDESTRIAN'S PACE

this cold bare room
with a few chairs and tables,
on the wall there is a clock,
it has stood the test of time,
in the day with people,
trampling in and out,
it moves at a pedestrian's pace,
on the night it remains on the wall
bewildered, like a star lost in space.

Mike Ridley (15)
Oundle and Laxton Schools

A STRANGE ROOM

A symmetrical but uneven classroom this is,
with the chairs in a line,
but with endless shapes around.
There's colour, pictures and objects around,
giving an atmosphere of warmth to some,
but claustrophobic to others.
It seems somewhat a wreck with
pieces thrown to the ground.
I would sort it out, clean up, and
create pleasure.
What things are hanging off the walls,
what mess there is on the desk?
I would sort it out,
I really would!

Roland Burton (15)
Oundle and Laxton Schools

THE WORST SET IN THE SCHOOL

The disruptive set
  We're just having a laugh
The ones that never work
  We just forget.
Objectionable, rude
  Just trying to be friendly!
You can't be bothered
  We're only Set D
Never concentrating
  Only bored

The worst set in the school
The worst set in the school.

N Criado-Perez (15)
Oundle and Laxton Schools

THE REDOING

Knocking back the door from a tree,
He entered nothing but a room of white painted stone,
He stood wondering,
Even with orders to begin,
He had a sack full of thoughts.

Then he started to gather his junk,
From bubbled glass to radiators of tangled steel.
The skylight windows were glass-filled,
Just like the open spaces to be filled with glass,
With glass above the door,
The fireplace was next to be laid.

Great slabs of marble were wheeled in,
All rusty and full of different shapes.
He chipped away.
In time lumps were flaking,
A larger picture of the peeling paint,
The fireplace was finished as was the carpet of orange.

Soon the room was finished,
Soon the room was begun,
Surely it had to be filled,
But with what?
'You, boy,' shouted the teacher.

Charles Parker (16)
Oundle and Laxton Schools

MAKING A COMEBACK

The mob is making a comeback.
The years of supposed peace
Are shattered by television and
front pages.

Which poses the question,
a comeback or just a new era
in its history. Will the old
fear of travelling return?

Are the police ready for a
comeback. Will their aggressiveness
return or has it always
been there those past years?

Just out of the spotlight,
in the dark where hooligans
search for the light and
with it recognition.

With recognition comes numbers
and back to the firms of
the eighties. The Cockney
with his blade.

Will a Saturday trip to
London ever be the same
again?

Felix Barnes (16)
Oundle and Laxton Schools

THE CLASSROOM

The grown-up walked into the classroom
and recalled how it used to be. In his childhood
memories he recalled the big wide open room
with the marble fireplace. He remembered the
skylights as they used to be with the sun
slowly filtering in.

His feet scraped across the carpet as countless
people's feet had done in the past. He remembered
how the chalk had screeched across the blackboard
and shook his head at the new gleaming
whiteness that now confronted him. As he looked
about he noticed the cracks in the wall and
remembered that a beast lived on the other side and
was trying to escape.

He felt a hand touch his and he looked down at
his son and said 'You have it soft these days.'
He turned and walked out the door leaving his son
staring at the room which had so enthralled
his father.

Chris Parsons (16)
Oundle and Laxton Schools

BABY

It's my baby.
It's my life.
So put me away.
Punish Baby's life too.

I may be wrong,
I may be compulsive.
So I break the law -
I'll do it again.

What do you think?
You hate the idea, don't you?
- Me as a mother.
Well face it - it's true,
Baby is mine.

Give Baby a chance.
I don't deserve one.
You can see me and my crimes
But see Baby - what crimes?

Catherine Cross (17)
Oundle and Laxton Schools

EVERY YEAR GETS HARDER

'Every year gets harder'.
Such a patronising line,
But the truth is not far off.

The system breeds naiveté,
Solid in personal thoughts,
We often reject the alternative ones.

History can prove our predictions,
If we only dare to look forward.
Is it worth the trouble?

We're in the past's future,
Where we live our fears,
But it's just reality.

And as we look back,
We curse ourselves,
And hold regret.

Olly Cooper (16)
Oundle and Laxton Schools

MY SAVIOUR

Sitting alone,
Feeling hopeless. Rejected.
My mind is submerged in memories.
I scream.
I feel only anger at the times which
were once my salvation.

I see images,
They haunt my existence,
Each turn becomes more frantic, until suddenly
I relax
I realise the only route out of this insanity.

But then it rings,
Calling out, drawing me,
I hear a friendly voice, soothing me, loving me -
I smile.
Life seems less daunting, I face up to the future.

Gemma Woodrow (16)
Oundle and Laxton Schools

PRESSURE

Creativity is surely something that comes by itself,
In darkest night, or at least on my own.
It can't be ordered, and I'm certain it shouldn't be.
It's a personal thing, and I can't be forced to share
My innermost thoughts with all these people.
It's not embarrassment, merely privacy.
A matter of choice.
And perhaps our Controller doesn't realise this.

Siân Gibson (17)
Oundle and Laxton Schools

A BROWN SOCIETY

Exposed to the real world without its cover,
The influence of today's society affects it.
It is a whole unit and is seen that way,
But it is versatile and is formed of individuals.
Each individual is elevated in unison,
However the exterior block of flats is crumbling.
The suburbs are not looking as good as they used to.
The centre is still intact as the nerve-centre of the area.
It is an American city composed of streets and avenues,
Each as relevant as the first. But they become,
Insignificant when hit by a natural disaster;
23rd is ripped in half as 24th is lost in the stomach of the earth.
When all is apparently finished, desolate and destroyed,
It still leaves a reminder of its former self, of its existence,
In the form of crumbs to stain its attacker's hands.

(Chocolate)

Simon Rowley (15)
Oundle and Laxton Schools

THE DIFFERENCE

No books, no teachers, no idea of what to do.
A blank piece of card, just a pen in my hand,
But surroundings seen a hundred times before:
The room is the same without the mobile phone.
Something not usually done, with music to inspire,
But none of it helps - what's the use of CDs,
With no knowledge of their histories?
What can be written on a bunch of flowers,
Stared at, but yielding nothing,
To the poets who look for ideas?

William Sankey (16)
Oundle and Laxton Schools

MADNESS

Like plague it takes us down,
Like AIDS it gives no sound.
It creeps up from within,
Like the vanquished give in,
We give in to madness.

Nothing we know
The process can slow
And we give in to madness.

Insanity	Madness
Vanity	Sadness
We all	give in

to
Madness

Jonathan Thakkar (15)
Oundle and Laxton Schools

JUSTICE

A problem that has interested man since the beginning
of civilisation.
It exists to civilise.
Justice and civilisation walk hand-in-hand,
but can't leave each other's sides.
Does it bring retribution to the victim -
or a punishment to the perpetrator?

Who are judges to decide the fate of an equal?
Are they not mortals of the same flesh and blood?
'Justice will be done' he says.
But what is justice, and how will it be done?

Andrew King (16)
Oundle and Laxton Schools

CHANGE?

Was I to write a poem,
About ten mushrooms and a mobile phone?
Surprise and confusion,
Has the art department moved upstairs?

Now, near silence . . .

A strange sense of unity's appeared,
Concentration's spreading, but to a few.
For those, the chocolate wanted eating,
And the music needed conducting.

Can no one accept a surprise, a difference,
A change without a reaction?

Annabel Lewis (14)
Oundle and Laxton Schools

COMPACT PAIN

Robert Johnson guitar on knee,
His false grin staring back at me.
Living in a black and white world
He's feeling blue and very cold.
'The Complete Recordings' Disc Two:
His life is shattered through and through.
His pressed pin-striped suit won't be worn again
Saffie walked out on him and into the rain.
The storm she left behind was empty of rage.
At home drops of pain spill onto the page.
His pen won't write, his fingers won't play.
They want him back in the studio later today.
As they take another film he sits and knows . . .
The second disc spells the end of this show.

Rachel Tracy (15)
Oundle and Laxton Schools

STRENGTH

N oises dart across the classroom as the strings march to and fro
$\qquad$ from the wall.
The tranquil wind section lags behind; merely drifting in a daze.
The phone lies silent though - asleep with the light off.
O utside the stone buildings peep at their neighbours and pry.
Watching the market folk set up stalls and . . .
Businessmen rushing along, concentrating on the phone.
K nowledge is the goal for which we all aim.
I know that I don't need that chocolate but . . .
My body's telephone is sending contradictory messages.
I nspired by an inanimate object to write this poem.
A black cuboid which is the size of my hand yet . . .
Nokia has the power to leap from Britain to Canada in seconds.
A ction as the end of our time approaches - the clock moves faster.
Fingers frantically scrabble for a pen.
The phone doesn't move but lies majestically still.
No need for action - its abilities say it all.

Jacqueline Hill (14)
Oundle and Laxton Schools

WINDOWS

They are there to let light in.
The curtains stop light escaping.
Don't be trapped in a room full of darkness,
For even he wouldn't keep you company.

Prisms emerge with blazing colours
On door knob, table, chair,
Little glints pick up the hints
In clean and shiny hair.

Yet with the light comes the darkness
To mingle with the birds' cheery song.
As we ask the question, the answer is plain -
Light's right and darkness is wrong.

So come out of the darkness,
Step into the light.
Open your window
And be gifted with sight.

Anna Wheeler (12)
Oundle and Laxton Schools

A POEM

Who are you, Robert Johnson?
I've never heard of you,
And why the random acorns?
(Picked up from chapel lawns)
Why must we all be made
To listen to this music?
Classical, people say they hate
And after this, I know why.
Two styles of music fight
But I'd honestly rather write
About that mobile phone
That reminds me of home.
But back to the acorns,
Perhaps they'll grow into a tree.
And as for Robert Johnson
On the cover of a CD;
Between you, I am torn,
And this classical horn.

Natalie Allan (15)
Oundle and Laxton Schools

PERIOD THREE

Things were different in period three today,
A change disturbed us, a change to the routine
Followed daily, caused muffled disturbance.
The familiar crescent of desks gave way to
Formal, coarse, separated plots.
People gather excitedly, inspecting objects,
On hard table-tops.
Chocolate in class, acorns, whatever next?
Music starts. Will the teacher below complain again?
I look around, catch someone's eye and smile.
Here a whisper, there a hurried scribble,
Caught by a sudden bout of inspiration,
Someone sits, distractedly.
Conducting the distant orchestra.
Now relaxing, a sense of enjoyment infiltrates the class.
All the while, the dull, milky light
Filters through the half-closed blinds . . .
And the rain-laden clouds scud by.
The music deepens with my mood as I listen
With dread.
For the coarse chiming of the break-time bells,
Breaking the spell.

Pippa Stevenson (15)
Oundle and Laxton Schools

SUCCESS?

What on earth are we doing,
Using this bizarre set of accepted ideals.
Sitting here, racking our brains
For something to ignite us,
Inspire us, to please teacher
While others far, far away or not so far,
Are in hopeless turmoil and unending despair.

We, the lucky few, have bounteous enough supplies
To use mushrooms, not as a source of nourishment,
But as a medium to conjure up images,
In our disorganised and deprioritised skulls,
So that we progress in our idea of 'success',
While others far, far away or not so far,
Are in hopeless turmoil and unending despair.

Alaric Shorter (17)
Oundle and Laxton Schools

FLOWERS

Given in romance, pardon or grief,
To show thanks or happiness,
Scenting a room with petal and leaf.

Brighten the garden, come sun or rain,
Giving colour to a room or a table,
Everyone loves them, fancy or plain.

As weeds in the grass, or blossom on trees,
A cycle of life with fresh buds each year.
Giving food for all insects and honey for bees.

All colours of a rainbow and mixtures of those:
From white to violet, violet to blue,
From peach to red, red as a rose.

All shapes and sizes, tiny white cowslips,
Sunflowers, huge, on trees and on bushes,
Poppies and tulips, all with their pips.

Given in romance, pardon or grief,
To show thanks or happiness,
Scenting a room with petal and leaf.

Francesca Dickinson (14)
Oundle and Laxton Schools

AUTUMN MOURNING

Pushing up through the smooth damp grass,
Innocent and white;
Touched by the soft autumn sunshine,
And damp morning dew.
But - severed at the stem,
They sit here steely cold;
Cut off before their prime,
They sit here motionless.
Seemingly peaceful -
They wait.

John Hart (15)
Oundle and Laxton Schools

A FOREST WITHOUT WORRIES

Relaxing and inviting a warm glow to encircle you,
Or perhaps it's a thick black cloud of mystery and magic.
An unsure feeling but one that arouses both carelessness and content
Like a spirit or like the sun, our anxious emotions have been eradicated.

The tinkling of the bells and the pitter-patter on the coarse skin
Like animals that are scurrying along the woodland in search of food.
Coming to play, looking for shelter from the big storm on its way,
As the trumpets blow, the rain pours faster and faster, the ground
wetter and wetter.

The soothing flute returns to ensure the little ones have been rescued
To save them from fear, to save them from death - it's alright.
Now it's peaceful, calm, tranquil like a flowing river so that
we can all be,
Painless, without worry, free, free, free.

Sonia Sangha (16)
Oundle and Laxton Schools

TRIVIAL SCRIPT

Boring. Intensely boring -
Most unoriginal - the, aid of
bore-merchants. Boring,
Still boring. And still: unclean.
As dead as its charisma,
As huge as its status - and
yet the cloud of boredom hangs
bringing with it ink-stained doom -
Education's symbol?

Mmm! Boring says the guiltless
consumer : served outdated
articles - boring bankers
brim with boring finds, lowly
exhibits, but all for some
dark-hidden purpose of gross
long-range relevance - in the
long-term perhaps we will know
why we all endured boredom
as on the face of that plane
a flat, lost world of fact and
of opinion - still boring.
Look now - boredom hovers but
his achievement is perhaps
great. 'Write twisted poetry!'
Bored yet? Wait till the writing
is ruined; lost? You'll need it.

Tom Rogerson (15)
Oundle and Laxton Schools

THE GIRL IN THE MUSIC

A ghost-like image
Clouded in mystery
Sitting at a window
Contemplates
the undercover tensions
that claw at her,
the cares that caress.
With her gentle warmth
contagious like a smile
she looks forward.
Her melodious hopes,
a flute's powerful song
sweet and pure.
The gentle longing spreads out from her
It roars sweetly across the room.
Her presence is felt,
not recognised.
But I know she's there
hiding in the music.
Obvious . . .
Discreet?

The music propels the image of this young girl,
It changes, she is lost . . .

Rebecca Hill (15)
Oundle and Laxton Schools

AN ATTEMPT AT SOMETHING

The sun grasps for effect through the blinds,
it wins, encircling his hair,
through the darkness of life,
it struggles not to be aborted.

Ricocheting like gunshot the inane tune enslaves me,
forcing me to appease my frustration
I have to hear it.

Gazing out, through barred windows,
the tree is ignited into action by the wind,
Outside life moves, has liberty and belief.
Indoors life and truth are stifled.

Life and value constrained like the wind,
Shut outside
like boats forced to travel where
they don't want to go.

The boat runs ashore, grounded
in both time and place,
until the tide of life returns,
to take it back to where it belongs.

Floating away alone and peaceful,
the sun rises,
the boy's face is lit up,
the girl can't see it,
the sea has released her.

Lucinda Leonard (17)
Oundle and Laxton Schools

THE ACORN

It falls through the branches,
Its smooth brown case shielding its fall.
More come with it,
Scattering the ground with shells.
Some are taken,
By birds and animals,
Some are buried beneath the soil.
They spread their roots thirsty for water.
They stretch their green solar panels.
Soaking up warmth and energy,
They push through the soil,
Spreading their branches into the sky.
And one day too, they will make
What they used to be.

Nicholas Proffitt (12)
Oundle and Laxton Schools

MUSHROOMS

They are furious,
White stubble shed to the ground, its downfall;
The fury of tiny bubbles soaring to a surface,
The violence of heavy boulders to kill and maim.

They are peaceful,
Innocent food feeding innocent mouths;
Little pebbles resting on a hazy sunlit coastline
The peace of a shadow cast in the midday sun.

They are magic,
A nation's craze for joy and happiness;
When always powerful, dangerous, yet oddly beautiful
When no one can tell their miseries or their smiles.

James Ducker (15)
Oundle and Laxton Schools

CHOCOLATE

I must write a poem.
As I look around the room I can see,
People writing, teacher in her chair and the,
cassette player, playing annoying music.

Think, Think!

The chocolate, the one on the table,
Its smooth, brown surface staring at me,
It looks so good and tasty,
I just want to devour it.

I want it, I want it!

No, the panic's setting in, what'll I write?
Come on think, think!
The chocolate, I can smell it, hear it calling to me.
No I must write a poem.

I must think, think!

There it is, the chocolate ready to eat.
I can almost taste it, can I have it?
No, this is important, I must write.
The chocolate, it's still on my mind, in my head.

I must think, think!
What'll I write, Write?

Ben Brown (12)
Oundle and Laxton Schools

CHOCOLATE

It stares at me and I stare at it,
Its purple wrapping peeled off as if
The blocks are trying to escape.
It whispers, 'Eat me, eat me!' but I resist.

Each block of chocolate is identical
And they are lined up in rows of four.
They are like apartment blocks
In a busy city.

They let off a rich aroma of cocoa
Another block of chocolate is seeming
To creep after the first also saying,
'Eat me, eat me!' . . .

Chomp!

John Saunders (12)
Oundle and Laxton Schools

THE MUSIC MAN

Pulses of electricity,
leaping from your music to my mind,
bathing my soul in shivering heat,
scoring fiery wounds down my back
making me writhe in delicious agony.
Notes, burning my white skin causing searing pain.

I want to drown in you,
rip out the breathing, bleeding soul in every line.
Feed on the emotions like an animal
find the mind behind the music,
and rape it like you raped mine.

I feel myself beg for you
you've got me helpless in your grip
I am *spellbound*, hopeless, lost.
I want to do the same to you,
I have to do the same to you.

Hannah Burch (17)
Oundle and Laxton Schools

OUTBURST

The soft, gentle rhythmic tune caresses the room
It twines with the scent of flowers.
As it dies down, there is a large outburst of flickering
Notes.
The lively rhythm relaxes and soothes my mind.
The gentle renaissance flows over me.
Nothing extravagant, but extraordinary.
It's as if you're floating in the clouds,
Nothing is going to disturb you, silence is surrounding every
Known secret place.
Creaking chairs are silenced.
A whole new world appears, everything comes to life.
All the feeling, love, hate, insolence drifts back.
The memories are everlasting.
Why didn't I know about this world before?
A secret place, where you can hide all your hated
Memories and bring out the love, and security that
Are your dreams.

Anna Dawson (13)
Oundle and Laxton Schools

MUSIC

Hypnotic,
Relaxing,
Soft choirs spiralling, swirling, spreading,
The room like a pool,
Soft notes as pebbles
Soundwaves lapping into every corner, cranny, crevice,
Caressing the room
Dancing
In
Space
Warm, bright,
Honey,
Flowing,
Slowing
Gone.

Joanna Murray (12)
Oundle and Laxton Schools

MY EXCUSE FOR NOT DOING LATIN

It had come to a choice,
Between learning Latin verbs
And writing a poem.
I wrote a poem.

Kate Anderson (12)
Oundle and Laxton Schools

TIME

My gaze lingers on the wall,
Transfixed by the dictator of my being,
The minutes of my life, slowly ticking away.
How ironic it is,
That a minute can mean so little, and yet hold so much . . .
This object, so bare and mechanical,
Controls my life to such an extent,
That I begin to despise and hate its existence.
Time is slipping me by,
Like sand through my fingers.
I grasp my hands tightly shut,
Trying to trap a few minuscule pieces,
Desperate to hold onto each and every piece,
To feel and experience every grain.
Yet, so much slips by me, unnoticed and insignificant.
Lost forever, in a vast plain of yellow and brown.
So often, I long for those hands to move quicker,
So often, I wish they would slow down.
Yet, so rarely do I ever stop
And think, about this moment in time?
Have I ever lived true happiness
And realised it there and then
And not years later,
Merely in reflection . . .
Too much time I spend planning and reflecting
So little, I spend acknowledging
My joy, or indeed sorrow.
Yet, what is the point
I am losing time,
For the hands never cease to turn . . .

Lya Pfaffli (17)
Oundle and Laxton Schools

MUSHROOMS

Mushrooms
Small and white
Round and smooth
Minding their own business.

Sitting so delicately, charming to behold
So easy to crush, looking so innocent
Harmlessly waiting to be eaten.

Yet when cooked and brown upon my plate
So evil they become
As I rebel and obstinately refuse
Point-blank to even touch them.

Even at six I'd made up my mind -
Mushrooms are ugly, distasteful, disgusting
The thought of eating fungus is truly revolting
Yet Mum and Dad don't seem to realise
How vile the little beasts are.

Dad laughs and scoffs one whole
It makes my stomach turn
So when Mum is distracted
And Dad disappears
Mine find their way mysteriously
Into the bin.

Jane Charlton (11)
Oundle and Laxton Schools

MUSHROOMS!

Mushrooms!
Cool, soft, pure, white.
Slight indentations, muddy skin
Peeling back, revealing beauty.
Pristine white, tender fibre
Edible.

Or fungi,
Dangerous, poisonous
Seemingly innocent
Lethal inside.
Never eat them, nor even touch them . . .
Inedible.

Two so different, but two so alike
One so delicious - the other - murder!

Rosanna Downes (12)
Oundle and Laxton Schools

THE MOBILE PHONE

It lies on the table all on its own,
Waiting for the next call to come.
It bangs into many things when it's not in use,
But now all alone.

It has a black plastic shell,
Which holds the inside in,
And keeps the outside out.
So blocks out all its fun in life,
And keeps it bored on its own.

Tim Dickinson (12)
Oundle and Laxton Schools

THE CHALK WEARER

My face can be as black as night but
sometimes can be white,
Meaningless words form on my face,
the amount that I learn is like a relay race.
Curious faces stare at me all day long.
I am often like a face of wisdom, teaching those
who sit before me, who still get it wrong.
I can see a door a table and a chair,
white chalky letters I always wear.
As the days go by my date always changes,
I am wiped with a cloth to reveal new pages.
I am always in rooms that seem like cages,
enclosing those who want to be free,
cleaned after every bell I will always be.
I see through the day and the night as well
and learn about those who learn what's on me.
The work's due in and I see people plea,
I see people grow and leave before me.
Once again the bell does ring,
and as children leave they seem to sing.
What am I, can you guess me?

Ashley Mitchell (14)
Raunds Manor School GM

LONELY MATTRESS

No one uses me
I am all alone
I wish I was back at my old home
I am all dusty and very fusty.

I can hear the odd car coming by
People talking and passing by
I wish I wasn't a bed and something else instead.

The room I am in is very dim
There is nothing else within
I am old and worn and slightly torn
I am not a pretty sight
So I will leave you now and wish you
goodnight.

Tom Cox (14)
Raunds Manor School GM

WAR

What is war?
Is it killing
Or is it sacrifice?
That is the question.

Who can take it?
Because I cannot.
Maybe in a couple
of years or two.

Will I come home
or die on the battlefield
trying to save my country
and all who live there?

Is it killing innocent people?
Or the thrill of using armoury?
But is it fun when dying
from serious wounds?

So what is war?
I will tell you,
It is suffering
and dying.

Stacey Barratt (12)
Raunds Manor School GM

THE TELEPHONE BOX

I stand alone on ceremony,
My red paint chipped,
My glass is smashed,
Meaningless words scribbled
over my face.

To you I blend into the background,
Although I notice every move you make,
Flash businessmen waltz by,
Lovers wrapped up in each other.

I hear everyone's secrets,
They don't realise I know,
People laugh, cry, gossip and shout,
These to me sound like thunder.

People gossip about others,
Blabbing about other people's secrets,
Laughing at the antics of 'supposed' friends,
Knowing they cannot hear a
word that is said.

Claire Woollard (14)
Raunds Manor School GM

WHAT AM I?

You tell me your secrets
In your dreams at night,
Lying in my sheets
Made of cotton so light.

You rest your head,
Upon my pillow
Closing your eyes
And drifting within.

You start to snore
It gets louder and louder
Twisting and turning
All night long.

As you twist and turn
In my sheets so light
You snore and dream
All through the night.

Kathryn Edwards (14)
Raunds Manor School GM

THE VIRUS

I am the virus, the cold, the flu,
turning someone's face from purple to blue.

I attack the lungs, the liver, the heart,
making someone's life fall apart.

I wander around this world of the red,
making someone uneasy and fall to the bed.

I eat and chew from the inside out,
organ to organ I continuously move about.

Oh no! An army of white things come chasing me,
I'd better go, hide, run away or flee.

I've got to get away,
or they'll somehow make me pay . . .

For all the damage that I've done.

Aaron Waller (14)
Raunds Manor School GM

MAN OR A MATCH

I sleep amongst identical friends,
Waiting for the moment of truth.
Laying peacefully like a resting squad
Soldiers straight and tall,
Pink heads waiting to be struck.

Faces straight, minds blank,
emotionally dead.
Rolling around with no control.
A dirty claw hooks out a fellow friend,
All emotions let loose,
Screaming like a jackal,
Never to be seen again.
The match is spent.

Grant Taylor (14)
Raunds Manor School GM

FROZEN TIME

I'm a frozen moment in time,
Framed by the growth of a tree.
I stand upon this box,
Which broadcasts news and weather.
A forever smile sits on my face,
My eyes full of laughter.
Behind me children play,
Snow falls from the sky.
However, I am warm
And cosy inside.
I'm a *frozen moment* in time.

Nicola Joy (14)
Raunds Manor School GM

RAINDROP

It hits me I'm heading for the floor,
I see my friends' faces drop as
they fall deep into the place that
seems like an ocean but is
just a few of my mates.
People keep jumping on me it's like
a screw being hit with a hammer.
I wish something or someone would just
come and suck me up, like a vacuum.
The sun comes out and I feel
myself disappearing, then suddenly
I've gone.
I'm no longer a raindrop,
I'm no longer a puddle,
I'm no longer myself . . .

Aimée Ryman (14)
Raunds Manor School GM

YOUR TELEPHONE

I sit in the corner doing no harm
  When all of a sudden you're pulling my arm.
I feel your finger in my stomach, a prod on my nose
  You're bending my wrist and pressing my toes.
Your shrill voice echoes down my ear
  'Oh well hello, how are you dear?'
I keep all your secrets, know all your ways
  Hear the gossip that everyone says.
I'm not your pet like a dog or a cat
  But I'm always here when you need a chat.
So whenever you're feeling sad or alone
  Just remember I'm here and pick up your phone.

Leanne Mayes (14)
Raunds Manor School GM

CLOUDS

Some say we're weak
Harmless and feeble,
Hardly a threat.

But we're unpredictable.
High in the sky,
Distant from all.

Infinitely picturesque,
We are the height of elegance
We will pose for a painting

And perform for our audiences,
But we are terrorists
To all that is living.

We command the rain
We command the snow,
We cast the shadows

On delicate fields of poppies
With little respect,
But abundant in power.

We are to blame for overcast picnics,
Endless dismal days
Appreciated but feared.

Developing our own style,
To control the weather
Is to dominate the earth.

Alexandra Fowler (15)
Raunds Manor School GM

SONNET - MEMORIES

Memories are stored inside our head,
They help us to learn from things gone wrong.
Without our thoughts we would all be dead,
With their help the road through life could be long.
Memories remind us of things done well;
They remind us of praise that we receive.
Memories can store sight, sound and smell.
Sometimes our mind starts to lie and deceive.
Fake thoughts can make us remember false things,
They teach us the wrong lessons.
True thoughts can make us rich with gold rings;
True memories teach us the best lessons.
Memories, memories help us through life,
They help us to live without too much strife.

Richard Barke (15)
Raunds Manor School GM

THE PILOT

My wings are now tired,
My wheels are now worn,
The oil in my cogs
Stops the grinding no more,
My radio has stopped,
I can no longer speak,
I'm doing the one-way flight,
That takes me to the peak.
As I land, the runway's white,
Ground control gave me such a fright.
My propellers have stopped,
              I am now dead.

Rachel Harvey (13)
Raunds Manor School GM

You

You walked into my life
Like a breath of fresh air
You looked into my eyes
With a loving stare.

You treated me the way
I was supposed to be
You made me feel happy and
You made me feel free.

You didn't care what your
Friends would say
You said we'd be together
Forever from this day.

You and me made one not two
You loved me and I loved you.

Andrea Childs (16)
Raunds Manor School GM

Cyber Pet Epitaph

I've got a little old friend which feeds, sleeps and can play,
I give it a call and it comes out today.
All kinds you can get, chicken, cat and dog,
You can toilet-train it by sending it to the bog.

My little friend has come and gone,
And the thoughts in my mind still linger.
I shall never forget the way I played with him,
And the way I used the littlest finger.

John Myers & Matthew Jarrold (13)
Raunds Manor School GM

YOU ARE THERE, WHEN YOU ARE NOT

A football match, a cricket match, a rugby match,
You are one of fifty thousand,
You are there but you are not,
A hospital waiting room,
You are there but you are not,
A garden, a forest,
You are there but you are not,
A town, a city,
You are there but you are not,
A different country
You are there, but you are not,
You think you are in many places,
Yet you are only in one,
It is the doorway to many worlds.

A Television

Scott Johnson (15)
Raunds Manor School GM

THE DENTIST

Every day he looked into people's mouths,
Some had big teeth, some had small.
He'd get the dreaded drill out and make a big hole
We screamed and shouted so he gave us a sweet
And we fell fast asleep.
We woke, were all drowsy, our mouths all dry
So he gave us a drink and shouted

'Bye bye!'

Hannah Carter (13)
Raunds Manor School GM

WAVES

The waves came crashing,
Breaking,
Rolling in,
Hitting the sand,
The rocks,
And your soul within.

You stand there,
Lonely,
Facing a sheer wall of power,
Rise up from the deep,
Making you,
Cower.

It's like a bomb exploding,
A tree falling,
A car crashing,
All in one.
The sheer size of the wave,
That great blue wall,
Makes you wonder where it's coming
From.

Matthew Hockridge (15)
Raunds Manor School GM

THE TEACHER

The desks are all empty,
The chairs are all still,
The books have all been
handed in,
Her presence is nil.

No more books to mark,
No more questions to be asked,
No more homework to be set,
Because now she is in the past.

Kelly Robinson (13)
Raunds Manor School GM

THE DENTIST

Who was that man leaning against,
that white wall
Working away on that pale face
on that grotty tooth?
The old painted fingers crept
through the patient's cold mouth.
The sparkly pale floor made a
clink when the tooth fell on the floor.
The bright large light would shine
into their eyes.

The seat would make a noise
every time they moved.
There would be silence until the
computer bleep every twenty seconds.
Blood would soak into the tissue.
There would be a slam.
Sweat was waiting to be wiped from
his forehead.
The instruments would be washed
then wiped ready for the next day.
The seat creaked, then a book slammed . . .
Silence was everywhere, nothing happened.

Hannah Cawte (13)
Raunds Manor School GM

REMEMBER ME ...

Remember me when nights are cold and grey as you draw comfort from the fire with a loved one.

Remember me on summer days that are warm and bright while I lie here all cold and dull.

Remember me with those steel eyes of grey and heedlessly forget the forlorn pain which I feel.

Remember me on outings of ecstasy with family sat around a spread of rainbow colours, good enough to eat.

Remember my relentless pain as you suffer insignificant quarrels with a loved one.

Remember me in days of good health and reflect upon these days that I have never had.

Claire Britchford (15)
Raunds Manor School GM

SHE LIVED HER LIFE ...

She spent her life as an
Intelligent brunette, trying
To control hyperactive
Children. In her hand were
Around twenty detention
Slips all ready to be
Filled out.
She had shouted and
Screamed and lost her
Voice but now she's
Silent and resting.
Goodnight Mrs Hesting.

Rebecca Farmer (14)
Raunds Manor School GM

THE ALARM CLOCK

I am the buzzer that drills
through your head
that keeps on drilling until you
wake up.
When you wake up I am normally
thrown because you are having
a very bad day.
When you have gone your mum
picks me up and puts me back on
the table.
When you get home you look at
me for the time and I just look
right back.
You see I'm very broken from
where I have been thrown.
And I just keep on ticking away,
'Tick, tick, tick!'

Jason Lovell (15)
Raunds Manor School GM

R I P

He used to love to see the moon, the sun
and the clouds. And in his occupation this
was easy for him. But now he is going to
see the clouds in heaven.

His job entailed staying at high altitudes.
Now he is as high as you can get.
He has gone and will be missed by
hundreds of passengers, and will be
missed by his family.

Ashley Burton (13)
Raunds Manor School GM

VERY PERSONAL COMPUTER

I spring into life as soon as he hits the switch.
My gigabytes giggling, my scanner scowling.

He stares into my face as if his eyes are stuck to me.
What's he looking at? It can't be that good.

He makes my letters feel like miniature punch-bags.
With huge pain,
While he's beating me up, I have to perform to him
like a Hollywood actor.

His fingers are the only moving part of his body which hover over and
around my keyboard.
He stops moving. He must be nearly finished.

I shout upstairs to the printers who rush frantically before ejecting the
work into a pleased hand.

I know he's going to switch me off like an unloved *machine*.

Steven Johnson (14)
Raunds Manor School GM

HAUTBOIS

My wind has stopped going down the tube
My keys have seized and rusted
And won't be pressed again
My joints are stiff.
My reeds have rotted and my pages are ripped
My clasp is loose and the lock is broken
My hinges have sagged
My case is broken
My stand has collapsed.

Michael Glover (13)
Raunds Manor School GM

LOOKING AT THE BIKE

Looking at the bike yes I'm ready to go
When looking even closer I thought it should be on show
I sit on the bike and pull back the clutch
I feel all the revs which excite me too much.

I pull down a gear and pull back the throttle
And boy, when I left I gave it some bottle!
It was so good that I gave it some more
I went into second and heard the engine roar.

I went so fast at top speed I did not care
And next minute I knew I was flying in the air
I hit the floor and took a long tumble
And when I saw the bike it was just one crumble.

But to this day I'm still a road hog
But when I had that accident I didn't 'arf need the bog!

James Watts (15)
Raunds Manor School GM

DOCTOR EPITAPH

This won't hurt a bit,
At least not anymore,
As no one could resuscitate him.
No one could find a cure.
'Dead on arrival' that's what they said,
Found on the floor lying dead.
He was his final patient,
The one he couldn't mend.
No pills or medicines could ever
bring him round.

Jillian Starkey (13)
Raunds Manor School GM

FOOTBALL

Whistle blows,
His heart beats,
His liver lets his blood flow,
He runs around for the ball,
His boots work until he falls,
The crowd cheer because he's scored,
It's Man U one, and Arsenal none,
The whistle blows,
It's half-time,
I wish the ref would just wait a while,
The whistle ends,
His heart stops,
His boots hung up tied in a knot
He's scored his last goal,
Had his last kick,
His fans no longer cheer,
because Cantona is no longer here.

Luke Wilmott (11) & Lewis Woods (13)
Raunds Manor School GM

EPITAPH - THE FIREFIGHTER

Here lies the body of Ben Biter,
Who was a very good firefighter,
He got burnt by a fire,
Turned round to a liar,
Got out his lighter,
And tried to fight 'er.
Now he lives in the life-after.

Craig A Hodge (13)
Raunds Manor School GM

A FOOTBALLER

His life was a rush
No Saturdays free
Out on the pitch at half-past three.

Training every month, every week, every day
Practising his skills just to make sure he'll play.

No time for his parents, family or friends
All the holidays he planned came to dead ends.

Ten thousand pounds he earned every week
Just for hitting a ball with his feet.

At that young age why did he go?
Where his plane crashed nobody knows.
All we can do is leave this here to remember him,
And light a candle and hope it never goes dim.

Goodbye!

Jamie Looker (14)
Raunds Manor School GM

DISC JOCKEY EPITAPH

Around and around my life has spun,
Reflecting in the light.
Being broadcast across the land,
Like adverts and bulletins.
For the final jingle has been played
And today's 'Top Ten' has been run down.
Today's and tomorrow's last song
                    was sung.

Becky Crews (13)
Raunds Manor School GM

WHY DID SHE LEAVE ME?

Why did we break up, I really loved her,
When she said goodbye, I wanted to die,
It was like the change of weather,
All it did was make me sit and cry.

I sat for hours and hours and thought why,
All I can remember is us at the seaside,
Every time I looked around I started to cry,
Then all of a sudden she had decided.

Her cheeks have a beautiful scent,
Her whole body smelt absolutely lush,
When she left me she left a dent,
When I first saw her I had a mind rush.

To my heart she was like a key,
I didn't want her to leave me.

Simon Merries
Raunds Manor School GM

IT'S A GAME

It's a game of dreams
It's a game of nightmares
It's a game of emotions
It's a game of pride
It's a game of passion
It's a game that keeps you on the edge
It's a game
It's a game of football.

Ashley Nelson (15)
Raunds Manor School GM

DEATH

Life after death's an unanswered question
Everyone wants to know but no one has found.
You die to know the answer to the question,
But when you die they lay you under a mound.
You can't speak and tell everyone what you've seen,
People say they see a bright shining light,
Hard to believe for I have not been.
Could it be that when we die it's like the night?
Some people think they know but how can they?
People can't die and later come back to life,
But then I could be wrong and they may,
But I don't believe that we have an after-life,
Life after death's an unanswered question,
And it will remain an unanswered question.

Chris Briggs (15)
Raunds Manor School GM

I LOVE THE WEEKEND

I love the weekend I think it's so cool
Compared to a school it seems like heaven.
Schooldays are hell teachers telling you what to do?
I wish it was the weekend all the way through.
If I had a choice there wouldn't be schools.
Wouldn't be teachers and there wouldn't be rules.
After the weekend it's back to school and all the rules.
Science is bad so is school.
But when we have practical I think it's cool.
The bell's gone and it's time to go.
It starts all over again and repeats itself five days a week.
Weekend again but it shall soon end, back to school and
back to hell.

Ian Parrott (16)
Raunds Manor School GM

LOVE

I saw her one day walking down the street.
She is more beautiful than I can see.
We walk miles and miles until we meet,
Sometimes I wonder if she's in love with me.
We share the stars and the moon together.
The clothes she wears are so unique.
Her beauty sometimes looks like the weather.
She smells as if she's on top of the highest peak.
Her long blonde hair and her big blue eyes
When she looks up she has a face like a cloud
They're almost as blue as the heavenly skies.
Her face is so rare, that's why I am proud.
I remember the first time we kissed
The love she gave me shall be surely missed.

David Barnes (15)
Raunds Manor School GM

A COURIER'S EPITAPH

He jumped in his van and zoomed off,
Not knowing where he would end up.
He sat in endless stand-stills,
Exhaust fumes filling the air.
Travelling miles with his A-Z and his
                    radio for company.
He went for miles to hand over a
                    simple package,
Not knowing when he would be home.
But now he has started a journey from
                    which he will never return.

Aimée Dickens (13)
Raunds Manor School GM

THE UNION OF MINDS

My love for you is never ending, dear.
It shines a light for me when I am down.
If you would leave I'd cry a final tear.
My tears would carry on until I drowned.
My heart beats love for you and no one else.
My life is not complete when you're not there.
Your beauty is worth more than any wealth.
No one could find a love that is as rare.
Each day my heart yearns stronger for your love.
I need you here to help me through the pain,
And take me to a place higher above,
Where love is like a breath you need to gain.
The union of our minds is like a song.
I wish our love to carry on and on.

Gemma Harness (15)
Raunds Manor School GM

A BLOODTHIRSTY CITY

A bloodthirsty city, daunting,
Excited from ghostly haunting
Intense juddering knocking loudly
Monster numbers overrun proudly
Quick run shouts terror
Unbelievable visions waking
              xenophobic yellow zombies.

Kara Friend (11)
Raunds Manor School GM

GLASSES

I hate my glasses they are so grim.
I hate the style of the big black rim.
I would like to put them in the bin.
But my mum would kill me and that would be a sin.

The teachers always tell me to wear them.
Sometimes I would like to stab them with a pen.
They sit on my nose like a pain.
I would like to kick them down the lane.

Sometimes I leave them at home
But then the teachers begin to moan.
Although wearing them is my target.
I'd rather sell them at the market.

I know that they are not that bad,
Although they make me rather mad.

Stuart Davison ((15)
Raunds Manor School GM

ANOTHER WORLD

I am the end of one world,
The beginning of another.
Look through the keyhole,
What do you see?
A place full of magic and surprises,
A wonderful place to be.
Only a lucky few may pass through me,
With smiles on their faces and stars in their eyes.
Bright colours, strange sounds,
Are what they hear and see.

As they push me open to enter my world,
They leave their sticky marks on my paintwork.
Stressed mothers follow their ecstatic children,
Quietly closing the door on the outside world.
Everyone leaves, the lights are turned out,
The magical world has come to an end . . .
Until tomorrow.

Tracy Haseldine (15)
Raunds Manor School GM

WHY SHOULD WE?

Why should we do our homework on time, eh,
Why should we do some extra work at school,
When we want to go to the swimming pool,
Or go to the farm and play with the hay?

Why should we go to school all the time,
Why should we do all our classwork on time,
I know that the work I do is not fine,
So why don't I go and do a simple mime?

Why should we all go on the boring school trips,
Why should we write about the trips when at home,
I don't want to go because I shall get hit,
I want to talk to my mum on the phone.

So why should we do all these nasty old things,
So why in the bath does the phone always ring?

Marc Hopkins (15)
Raunds Manor School GM

MY BOYFRIEND

My boyfriend made me sit at night and cry.
I loved him in every way but one.
I just didn't want to say that word goodbye.
Loving him can be so much fun.

I sit and wait for him to phone.
As I'm left waiting time goes by.
The phone never rang, I was alone.
I don't know why he has to lie.

I decided to go for a long walk.
I sat down and began thinking.
In the end I decided we should talk.
When I was talking he kept blinking.

When we argue I always seem to win.
As long as he is mine I love him.

Julie Parkin (15)
Raunds Manor School GM

ANGEL

The stage is still
The lights are off
The act she lived has now been stopped
Her life was one long masquerade
but now the veil she wore has dropped.

Each time she danced into the spotlight
The nation's eyes upon her
Her feelings masked with a joyful show
of love and fun and comfort.

Her eternally happy smiling face
that embraced so many souls
Now those creatures are left behind
with infinite unfinished roles.

She would glide across the floodlit floor
With beauty blonde and bare
Why did God have to take her?
This life is so unfair.

She was a visiting angel
So beautifully blessed
But now she is just a memory
May her soul forever rest.

Lucy Marland (13)
Raunds Manor School GM

THEY SAY TIME IS THE FIRE . . .

They say time is the fire in which we burn,
And death is the one constant in this lonely world.
If we ever escape we have yet to discern,
At the end of this existence into hell shall we be hurled?

Will the mouth of death come and eat me up?
Will I lie in darkness where nothing occurs?
Will the grim reaper come and poison my cup?
Will someone walk over me saying 'That grave is hers'?

Or will they all live beneath my cloud of joy,
Not knowing where I am or how to get there, too?
Will I exist in a place where evil has no ploy,
And love touches everyone not just a few?

Is time a predator that stalks us all our lives?
Or a companion to cherish, in your eyes?

Gabrielle Evans (15)
Raunds Manor School GM

SEE YOU IN HEAVEN

I need to see you in heaven, because
I never told you how much I loved you,
And now my time has come and we are through
The gates have opened up for me up there,
And when I get there I will do the same,
You have been good to me until this day,
I want to say 'I love you' but don't know how,
I know that one day I will meet with you,
Waiting for the day you come to join me,
I hope you are not too lonely down there,
I am watching over you, dreaming of you,
I can't wait until our re-uniting day.
Then you and me will always be together.
That is the day that I am dreaming of.

Emma Davis (15)
Raunds Manor School GM

I SAW YOU STANDING THERE

I saw you standing there,
for the first time,
I never thought that
you would ever be mine.

I saw you standing there,
looking at me,
Now I know why they say
the best things are free.

I saw you standing there,
with your loving blue eyes,
I dread the day when
we have to say our goodbyes.

I saw you standing there,
all innocent and sweet,
Just the thought of you
makes my heart skip a beat.

I did see you standing there,
just one minute ago,
But now I don't see you,
Where did you go?

Nicola Stillman (15)
Raunds Manor School GM

MY LOVE FOR YOU

My love for you is a beautiful thing.
I hope we will share all of our lives together
The days go on, everlasting.
Our love is strong and will last forever.
You are my moon, my stars, my sun
I wish we could run away to our own island
Where I wouldn't have to share you with anyone.
We would sit arm in arm, hand in hand.
If my love for you was rain it would relieve a drought
Your every wish would be my command.
You could have everything you've ever dreamt about.
You make me the happiest man in all the land.
So one wish I ask of you in return,
Is that like a candle our love will always burn.

Holly Morgan (15)
Raunds Manor School GM

EVER-FRIEND

We came so close, at first I didn't know,
As you helped me to find my way, walk through the rain.
I should've seen, sometime you'd have to go
And leave me there alone with all my pain.
Although I know that it was not your fault,
It was not fair, I blamed you all the same.
Over troubles, together we would vault,
It was so easy for us, it was like a game.
We shared completely everything we had,
Though we only wanted friendship of the mind.
Love of the bodies would be bad,
So as friends we'd search and see what we could find,
But now I feel like I have lost a friend,
I look deeper, our friendship could never end.

David Noakes (15)
Raunds Manor School GM

THE FOG

Everywhere you look, and
Everywhere you go, your
View is blocked.
Everything is blurred.

It's very cold and misty,
You can never touch it,
Almost taste it.

Four great grey walls, like towers.
It's dull and hazy.
It lurks low, but
Everywhere you look it blocks
Your vision.

Everything's silver, all around you.
You can feel it, like water vapour
Creeping and lurking about.

When you breathe you can see
Your breath
Which disappears into the
Misty, hazy
Dewy, dull
Slow clouds of,
Fog!

Michael Aird (15)
Raunds Manor School GM

WINTER

Winter is the time when you wrap up warm,
The snowflakes come and the icicles form,
The children make snowmen with hats on their heads,
Waiting for Santa, tucked up in their beds.
The children wake up on Christmas Day,
To open their presents and start to play,
Meanwhile outside the snow is falling down,
Covering the rooftops in every town.
The robins hop around in the snow,
Leaving their footprints wherever they go,
Everyone is playing and having fun,
Although it is cold and there is no sun,
The winter ends when the snow disappears,
The sun comes out and the warmth of summer nears.

Luke McLellan (15)
Raunds Manor School GM

INSIDE LOVE

Our love was so short,
It was all taken away,
Your silly games made it happen this way.
Our only communication is a pen
on a piece of paper.
Why is it so hard to write 'See you later'?
If I was to ever see you again
I could only caress your face and hands.
The big steel bars come between us;
It makes me feel like we're in separate lands.
I just can't stop remembering
The way you held me close,
Almost safe;
The way you would whisper sweet nothings
in my ear.
Now there's nothing,
Just barriers.
I can't stand the pain
As I am slowly going insane.

Ashley Scott (16)
Raunds Manor School GM

THE MUSICIAN

My wooden body is broken.
My varnish has worn off.
The strings on my bow are loose.
My music is no longer of any use,
But I know that once I was the best,
Now my body has been laid to rest.

Gemma Strange (13)
Raunds Manor School GM

IN THE CITY

All day fumes from cars splashing in my face
Buildings as tall as a giant
Children scattered wherever you look
Dogs abandoned by their hateful owners
Everyone stuffing themselves with fish and chips
Families everywhere around the city
Ghostly houses that are no good anymore
Hungry children who are begging for money
I absolutely hate the noise in the city
Joe and John are playing happily in the park
Keyboard and other musical things in the shop window
Lots of lorries cars and buses zooming past
Mobile phones ringing all the time
Noses sneezing all day long
Over the city is a lovely countryside
Patrol cars looking if there are any robberies
Queues in shops miles long
Roaring engines trying to start
Sad people never come out to play
Two big buses stop to pick people up
Underground tunnels leading to trains
Valuable things all over the museum
Woken up by the cars whooshing past
X-raying people in the general hospital
Yapping yells coming from children
Zebras being stroked in the zoo.

Michael Patterson (11)
Raunds Manor School GM

PICTURE

Alcohol abuse
Beggars on street corners
Car theft
Dogs' mess everywhere on pavements
Exhaust fumes
Factories making pollution
Graffiti on shop walls
House burglary
Illegal drugs
Joyriders all about the street
Kids fighting in the street
Lights flashing at pelican crossing
Motor cars on the busy roads
Noise pollution
Old factory buildings still half-standing
Public transport
Quiet libraries that people go to
Rubbish all over the pavements
Sirens (police cars, ambulances)
Traffic jams
Under the bridge tramps sleep
Vandalism in parks
Window smashed in shops
X-rays in hospitals
Young children going to church on Sundays
Zebras in zoos that people go and see.

Leanne Kennedy (11)
Raunds Manor School GM

NAN

She used to sit me on her knee and tell,
The stories of her life when she was young,
They were so vivid, I could even smell,
The flowers that she used to sit among.
She used to tell the garden all her thoughts,
The trees would whisper through the balmy air,
She said she loved to run and play all sports,
Sometimes I really wish I had been there.
The chair in which she used to sit is bare,
It won't be replaced for one that's new,
The image of her face, her hands and hair,
Will stay with me until I pass on too.
The happy memories of Nan live on,
She used to cheer me up, but now she's gone.

Sam Francis (15)
Raunds Manor School GM

THE SMALL BOY IN MY STREET

As I watch from my highest window,
I always see this small young boy.
His hair is brown to match his eyes,
with a small baby face and little pink ears.
He has a tiny mouth, but a smashing smile.
He winks at me and walks away.
As I watch him leave the street,
he walks half-way,
then runs the rest
until I can no longer see him.
Back in the street the road is clear,
the sun's gone down,
the lamps are bright.

Audrey Albert (12)
St David's RC Middle School

A LITTLE VOICE

Nobody listens to a word I say, I think I'm
                a ghost in total mid-air.
Nobody, but nobody, listens to a word I say.
I told these children to stop now running,
                but still no reply.
Nobody, but nobody, listens to a word I say.
As I stand in the playground all on my own,
I wonder, I wonder what to do.
Nobody, but nobody, listens to a word I say.

Nobody, but nobody, will ask my name.
Nobody, but nobody, takes notice of me.
Nobody knows how I feel inside.
Nobody, but nobody, will listen to a word
                I say.
I feel so useless and I feel so thick, that
nobody, but nobody listens to a word I say.

Caroline Wieczorek (13)
St David's RC Middle School

PERCUSSION

D rums drums listen to the beat
R umble rumble
U nder your feet
M ums yelling stop, stop, stop.

K eep it going
I t's so hot
T he sound is hot so I just don't stop.

Tom Curtis (12)
St David's RC Middle School

INTO SPACE

Into space now we go
Not for ever, no, no, no!
To the planets now we go
Over the moon go with the flow

Space, space is a very big place
Pluto Neptune Jupiter Mars
All the planets and all the stars
Galaxies far far away
In the space shuttle now I play
Planets, planets everywhere
I look out watch and stare
Comets coming from every place
End our journey now through space.

Jermaine Marcano (13)
St David's RC Middle School

AUTUMN

The leaves fall off the trees,
With their golden colours glowing,
They slowly flutter in the warm breeze,
Without anyone knowing.

They swirl and whirl up in the sky,
So beautiful and frail,
They move around like a butterfly,
Then fall to the ground like a snowflake so pale.

They crunch and crackle on the ground,
While the small children are playing,
All the people are now around,
All the leaves are down softly, laying.

Emma Garratt (12)
St David's RC Middle School

FIREWORK NIGHT

Tonight's the night, the sky's alight.
Flashes and sparks go through my ears and eyes.
My little sister tells a lie,
I get so mad I flash, crash with temper and cry.
All of a sudden I hear screaming in the sky.
What could it be? It's Firework night! *Bang!*
I call my sister a liar
My dye disappears from my hair.
I go to the toilets and with shock my hair is pure grey.
I am only twelve years old.
Oh, why does this have to happen to me?
So I cry and cry for five years until I find out that it is
five-year paint-laster. Oh I am so, so happy,
I tell a joke.
On the 5th of November there are always sausages.

Splashed paint and bangers and beans!

Cathleen McHugh (12)
St David's RC Middle School

POEM

I can't write poems,
I think and think
But there's nothing there,
It is so hard to write.

Everybody writes,
But my paper stays white.
My mind is blank,
I just can't write.

I cannot rhyme,
I write the worst poems,
I stay up all night
But I still can't write.

I've never been able to write
Anything that is right,
Sometimes I give up,
I know it's too hard.

Sean Cassidy (13)
St David's RC Middle School

A HEAVENLY PLACE?

My mind drifted far and deep,
To a place where souls keep
Their remembrance, their past lives,
Mothers, fathers, children, wives.

Pity in their eyes, their lives have gone,
No more sorrow,
No more joy,
No more anger,
No more wrong.

Cruelly parted from their years,
        Remembrance of happiness,
        Remembrance of tears
Missing the family they only had,
        What had they done that was
                            so bad?

Catherine Fitzsimons (13)
St David's RC Middle School

DEATH

An unbearable flame, burning within me,
Scorching my soul, draining it empty.
A monstrous sound, that drags on and on,
I screw up my eyes and wait till it's gone;
But then I realise this painful, whirling madness,
that excludes me from feelings of joy or sadness,
will stick like glue and leave me never.
This anguish and emptiness will trap me forever.
All my memories before me flickering,
Of playing, working and silly bickering;
And then I feel lost and scared,
Death has caught me in the coils of its snare,
Claws lash at me, a mass of knives,
Carving away my empty soul, taking my life.
A rush of wind as I rise through the sky,
Everyone I've known up here so high,
Then all that I've had, all that I've found,
Ripped away suddenly, as I'm pulled to the ground.
All my energy, all my strength,
pumped up strongly from my inner depths,
I can feel the power, I can see the light,
I won't go to hell without a fight.
The eternal flames of hell, burning me whole,
Taking my body but freeing my soul.
I soar through the sky to the radiant glow,
Joy and peace fill my soul,
The tranquil feeling calms my fears,
Up here in heaven my mind is clear.
Meeting people who have died before me,
Rejoicing at these wonders for all eternity.

Edmund Preston (12)
St David's RC Middle School

DESERTED

Lost and alone, I don't know
where I am.

The windy skies and the
golden sand.

Dreams no longer mean anything,
to my heart or mind.

Never knowing what I
might find.

I miss my family and
my friends

Will I stay out here . . .
                    it depends . . .

Abigail Gaughran (12)
St David's RC Middle School

ABSEILING

Climbing to the top,
I really want to stop.
40 foot high,
I think I'm gonna die.
Shaking like a leaf;
Scared beyond belief,
Hitch up to the rope,
Step backwards down the slope.
            Over and down.
Petrified. Jelly legs,
Then I'm safely on the ground.
Can I do it again?

Heather Isaksen (12)
St David's RC Middle School

IT'S A MYSTERY . . .

The sun was setting in the sky,
And calm set all around,
As the ocean lapped onto the shore,
A silhouette was found.

It was one of a teenage girl,
Who was slim and very tall,
She stood upon the ocean shore,
Quite obvious to all.

She was upon the warm grey rocks,
And the wind ran through her hair,
As she looked into the ocean,
A soft and friendly stare.

Slowly her legs changed,
And they joined together,
They turned into a tail,
Which would be forever.

She dived into the sea,
And went down beyond view,
Down, down, down,
From an old world to a new.

What happens next nobody knows,
Or where she is or where she goes,
Her life is now in the hands of the sea,
Away from humans like you and me,
Wherever she goes it's a mystery,
It's a mystery, it's a mystery . . .

Marie McLoughlin (12)
St David's RC Middle School

NIGHTMARES AND DREAMS

Dreams are nice and fair
but nightmares give you a scare
and sometimes in a nightmare you
can be chased by a bear.
So here is what you do
just to make it fair
you go over to dreamland
and get another bear.
Dreamland is an excellent place
you can do what you like
you can go to the shops
and get the latest bike.
My favourite ones are dreams
when I go to bed because you
can never get buried when you're
                            not dead.

Levy Chandler (12)
St David's RC Middle School

RIFLE SHOOTING

Out in the open with the morning dew
Target 50 yards away
Tension mounting adrenaline flowing
Slowly squeezing, squeezing, jerk and bang.

Sweating with the noise of my last shot
Sight adjusted aimed at the bull's eye
No jerking just the slightest pressure *Bang!*
200 mph the pellet travels
Then makes contact
              Bull's Eye!

Edward Mattacola (12)
St David's RC Middle School

RAIN

The sound of rain splattered above
And made me feel in the mood
                        for love.
The smell drew near as the clouds
                        appeared,
And made the surroundings seem
                        clean and fair.

The comforting joy
It brings for us all,
When we stay in at home,
Where all is warm.

Some droplets are big,
Others are small.
Some will fall in a river,
Others will make you shiver.

The sun appears
Once the clouds have gone,
And keeps its shine,
Until the night has come.

Alina Lawrenson (12)
St David's RC Middle School

THE CAT

The cat lay peacefully on
the rug next to the fire.
His black fur shone in the light,
the fire blazed,
as the radio played.
The cat opened his eyes and
softly purred,
he slowly got up and
stretched out his powerful
hind legs and his sharp claws.
Cats scare me so badly
I even think that they're there
when they're not,
I wish I could erase them
from my mind,
But I can't.

Christina Yarborough (12)
St David's RC Middle School

THE GLASS WINDOW

The glass window is all so plain,
No one to talk to and no one
to play with,
No one to share how it's thinking
or feeling
but maybe one day it may have
some colour.

Sarah Porter (12
St David's RC Middle School

BUMP IN THE NIGHT!

I lay in my bed
one cold pitch-black night
When a scrape on the window
woke me up with a fright.
Who's there? I shouted
but there was no reply.
Scrape! Scrape!
The sweat gushed down my
goose-bumped chest.
Should I shout for my mum
or would he hear me?

> *Oh*
> > *no!*
> > > *He's*
> > > > *coming!*

Where shall I hide?
Maybe if I don't move
he won't see me.
Too late, he's seen me,

Why me? Why me?
> *Take the reader!*

> > *A r r r r r g h!*

Ryan Hodges (12)
St David's RC Middle School

ASTHMA

Asthma is good,
Asthma is bad,
People are happy,
Then people are sad,
I have bad asthma
And get picked on,
People don't really like me.
When I am sick,
When I am bad,
My real friends
Help me like
Lizzy and Tara,
But most of my
    family help too.

Natalie Cooper (12)
St David's RC Middle School

RUNNING AWAY!

I often think of going away to a new and far place,
I decided I'm going to pack my case.
I'm gonna walk the streets not knowing where to go,
I'm gonna walk the streets searching high and low.
Who knows what I'll come by?
Who knows where I'll lie?
I'm going away and I'm sure I'll shed a tear,
And I know it's the right thing to do,
And I know I'll miss you.
When I finally get the courage I'll phone,
When I finally get the courage
    I'll no longer be alone.

Suzanna Campbell (12)
St David's RC Middle School

WITCH, WITCH!

A town of suspicion,
      Chanting low whispers of hatred.
Wishing me dead,
      For sorcery is against
            their faith.
So they rest me upon a stake of wood,
And ere me a pile of twigs and sticks
      and branches to burn for now,
            It's my turn.
I will never forget the devil, dancing upon my
shoulder that night, as he cloaked me.
How I bared the blazing light, and my soul,
It rose into the black, gothic clouds of hell.
The glare of the minted moonlight's atmosphere,
Glistening in my eyes, is imprinted in my mind forever.
My relics are buried in this
      sepulchre of deep slumber,
            to be forgotten.

      You are now insightful to my life.

Emma O'Donovan (13)
St David's RC Middle School

I CAN'T HEAR YOU

I am deaf,
But I am not thick,
I just can't hear very well.
I'm just deaf.

I wear hearing aids to help,
I'm a brilliant lip-reader,
I use my eyes instead of my ears,
And all my friends help,
Because I'm deaf.

It is not too bad to be deaf,
Because people pick on me,
But that might be because I'm small,
And not because I'm deaf.

Elizabeth Zannino (13)
St David's RC Middle School

SLAVE

The happiness, the sun shining.
All the hills, the trees for climbing.
Broken in half, darkness around,
Everyone falls to the ground.
Captured,
Taken,
Stolen,
Gone,
No one left,
Take everyone.
Squashed and crushed and
Starved and weak.
Dirty water running past
My feet.
Sold and bought for people's
money.
Weather terrible, not even
sunny.
Taken somewhere, worked
like a slave, whipped or
punched if I misbehaved.

Dana Hogan (13)
St David's RC Middle School

THE SKUNVARK

The ant-gobbling striped skunvark,
Owns a tail that gives off a rotten crude smell,
The terribly ugly skunvark,
He's the creature from the depths of hell!

People can smell him from twenty miles away,
He drives them completely insane,
The skunvark kills hundreds every day,
Britain wishes he never came.

When he was first discovered, people would stop and stare,
They would watch the animal with the pink and green
                                        stripy hair,
And when the crowds grew and grew,
The disgusting smell began too,
The bright colours were meant to warn people away,
By not taking notice they would now pay.

Everyone choked, they fell,
They suddenly all died,
It was because of the gruesome smell,
And then the skunvark sighed,
His torturers have now died!

Ian Gould ((12)
St David's RC Middle School

FORGOTTEN

Tears of blood crash to the floor,
As cries of pain echo around the room.
Darkness is just a way of life,
Loneliness her only companion.
All her loved ones given up hope.
Alone,
She's just a shadow,
Soon to be forgotten.

Thoughts of hatred fill her mind,
No room for fear.
Alone she sits,
Alone in darkness.
Never to see the light of day.
Alone and forgotten.

Sam Loughrey (12)
St David's RC Middle School

THERE'S A MONSTER IN MY BED

There's a monster in my bed
I can hear it rumbling
There's monster in my bed
I can see it tumbling.

There's a monster in my bed
I wonder if it's small?
There's a monster in my bed
I bet it's very tall!

There's a monster in my bed
I know it's not a fairy
There's a monster in my bed
I think it might be furry.

There's a monster in my bed
I know it's after me
There's a monster in my bed
I'll get Mum to come and see!

There's a monster in my bed
I'd better fetch my bat
There's a monster in my bed
Oh Mum! It's just the cat!

James Timmons (12)
St David's RC Middle School

AN ANCIENT BARD

On a very still night
When the world is flooded with moonlight,
Don't go down to the old graveyard,
For there lies the body of an ancient bard.
When the moon is full
And the farmers gather at the Roaring Bull,
Don't go down to the old graveyard,
For there lies the body of an ancient bard.
When the witches fly
And the stars cover the great, black sky,
Don't go down to the old graveyard,
For there lies the body of an ancient bard.

And on nights like this
When the moors are flashing with will-o'-the-wisp
He rises up from his ancient grave
And steals the souls of the lurking brave
Who, watching over the old stone wall
Have come to see if tales tall
Of the ancient bard are true.

And with fingers gently strumming,
Upon his golden harp,
His lilting music fills the air,
And people living for miles around
Shudder at its eerie sound.

Joanne Osborne (12)
St David's RC Middle School

SOMEBODY LISTEN TO THE REAL ME

I may be big,
I may be tall.
I may be short,
I may be small.
I may be fat,
I may be thin
I may have dimples on my chin.
I may be quiet,
I may be shy
Sometimes I'm upset
And want to curl up and die.
I feel like people are laughing at me
I don't know why.
I know I'm happy, inside of my heart
My contentment and love
Cannot be torn apart.
No one will give me the time of day,
To ask how I'm feeling
Or if I'm okay.
Inside my heart there's a whole new me
Suppressed in this body!
I want to be free!
Sighed 'Me'!

Emma Mandley (12)
St David's RC Middle School

THE SPECIAL TREE

Sycamore trees
Reach for the sky.
So do the oak, elm and yew.
But below them, there is
A tree that doesn't
Care for the sun in the sky.

Its fragile limbs
Can't hold its weight.
It droops, its bark is bent.
No bird can nest there,
And all the insects are
Aware that this tree is special.
It gazes at its reflection
All day long, it worships water
Not the sun.

Charlotte Rampley (12)
St David's RC Middle School

GHOSTS

Ghosts, ghosts!
They're not so clean,
They're a bit of a death machine,
They come at night when the lights ain't bright,
And scare the humans that might have frights,
They're green and blue and yellow too,
They're mean and nasty
                    and want to be seen.

Chris McGuigan (12)
St David's RC Middle School

THE WHITE LADY

Waves crash upon the shore,
Over the place where a young girl walks,
Wandering, searching for her loved one,
Her lost one who never came,
Her white gown is flowing,
Her long hair streaming,
She is at peace with the world.
But tears sting her eyes,
She is a creature of the night,
No longer a being, or a part of life.
But what is this?
Footsteps behind her!
Creeping, crawling, watching over her.
She turns with fear in her eyes.
'Tis her loved one, come from the grave,
And now, she is running, following the footsteps,
But alas, he is gone, lost forever.
Hatred in her eyes of glass,
As she takes the evil blade,
And with one move, one jerk of her hand,
She falls, falls to the ground.
She is gone, gone forever,
To be reunited with him,
          In harmony, in love, in peace!

Sophie Foster (13)
St David's RC Middle School

FREEDOM!

Freedom is something that I haven't got
I'm stuck here like glue and just starting to rot.
No one will visit me and that's because
I'm starting to smell like a dead body does.

I'm locked away from the outside world,
Sitting on the floor all withered and curled.
Crying all morning all day and all night
As I sit there in darkness without even a light.

I just want my freedom, that's all I need,
No drink, no blanket, not even a feed.
So please give me my freedom and let me be free,
To get out of this room, *just give me the key!*

Natalie Leney (12)
St David's RC Middle School

THE WEIRD WONDER

I feel a tingle down my
spine, I think it's a weird
wonder of mine. I look
behind and then I see, a
poltergeist following me

It looks real weird for
a ghost, it reminds me of
when I walked into a
lamppost, now it's all
blurred I cannot see
the weird wonder in me.

Lee Cooper (11)
Wollaston School

CRIMSON

The captains sat in the captain house,
They spoke in voices quiet as a mouse.
And in every scabbard, on every belt,
Was a sword with a crimson blade.

The knights patrolled the battered walls,
On one side the fields, the other the halls.
And in every scabbard, in every belt,
Was a sword with a crimson blade.

Horses trod the fallen down,
Into the mud that was red, not brown.
And on every scabbard on every belt,
Was a sword with a crimson blade.

One man led these weary men,
And they should have left him then,
For in his scabbard, upon his belt,
Was a sword with a bright, clean blade.

David Clements (12)
Wollaston School

THE WONDERS OF SPAGHETTI!

As I slid down the cold glass jar,
I was hard and then I *snapped!*

I softened out of my hard shell,
The wonders of spaghetti are just *unthinkable!*

Helen Gant (11)
Wollaston School

WHEN THE MAGIC HAS GONE

Christmas was magical when I was young,
Every second was filled with fun.
As I looked around,
Every face wore a smile,
It was all so exciting when I was a child.
Santa visited my home every Christmas Eve,
That's what they told me, that's what I believed.
One day I stopped believing,
Then the magic was gone,
Santa's mince pie stayed in the tin where it belonged.
All the excitement somehow disappeared,
It gets a little less special every single year.
Hold on to dreams of Christmas
Because it won't last long,
And it will never be the same,
When the magic has gone.

Kate Cosford (15)
Wollaston School

MY FRIENDS

My friends are cool
My friends are kind
My boyfriend is so fine.

My friends make up my mind
My friends are supportive
My friends are the
best!

PS . . . Better than the rest anyway!

Laura Gorman (11)
Wollaston School

THE GREAT EXPRESS

The train was running along the track,
Everyone is looking back.
Leaving their homes,
To a great big city,
A city that is really busy.
The train had a special number
The number '1',
The people on the train had lots of fun,
As they were thinking of the shops
The train suddenly stopped.
There they saw a great big station,
Lots of people handing in their tickets.
There they saw a bus to take them,
On they got and went.

Kerry Bates (11)
Wollaston School

FIRST THOUGHTS OF WOLLASTON SCHOOL

As I made my way out of bed,
The thought of being the smallest came into my head
I gave a yelp as I touched the floor and made my way
over to the door.

I quickly got ready for school and then down the stairs
and into the hall.
Out the door and into the street,
Only hearing the sound of people's feet.

Nearer and nearer to the bus stop I get,
Seeing my new friends I have only just met.
Suddenly the bus is here,
People looked at me as I gave a big cheer.

Keri Boyles (11)
Wollaston School